NORWAY'S STAVE CHURCHES

Architecture, History and Legends

NORWAY'S
STAVE CHURCHES

Architecture, History and Legends

EVA VALEBROKK

THOMAS THIIS-EVENSEN

TRANSLATED BY:
ANN CLAY ZWICK

BOKSENTERET

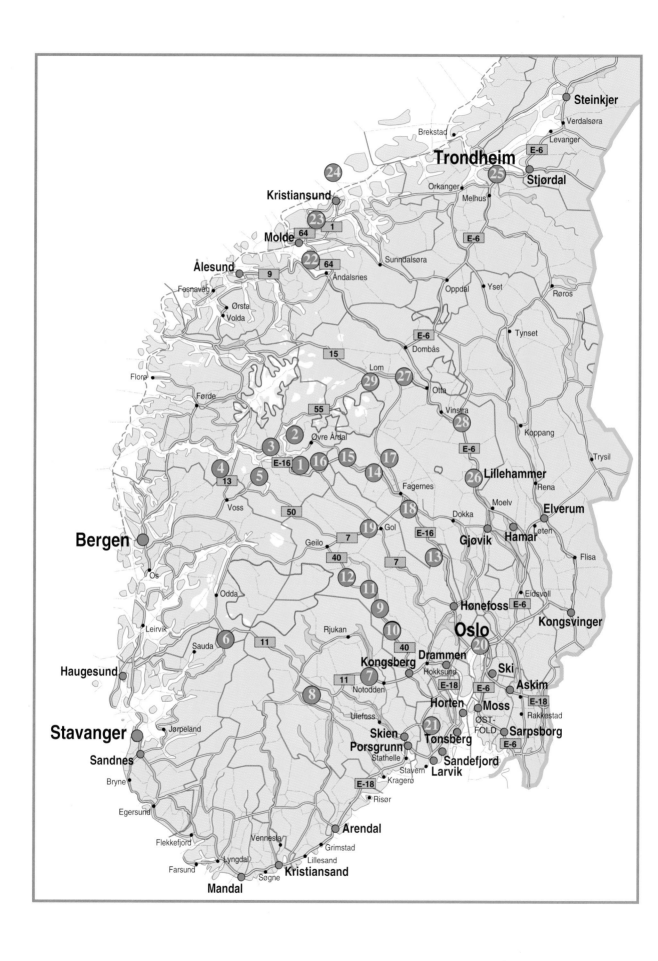

CONTENTS

EXPERIENCING A STAVE CHURCH

BY THOMAS THIIS-EVENSEN

A STAVE CHURCH. In the hearts of Norwegians, these very words bring forth a wealth of associations. Tightly packed into this dark, small building is our entire history, lying dormant in a juxtaposition of the Viking Era and Christianity. Its columns and ridge turrets, carved dragon decorations, and durability display a technical skill that is as amazing as it is impressive. As a place of worship, these churches were "messages in wood": each column and plank was erected in God's honour and in praise of the "White Christ" who drove Odin and Tor from their valleys and fjords.

Scattered throughout the country, along routes of trade and paths of pilgrims, as many as 900 of these "dark messages in wood" accompanied the traveller on his journey.

By visiting the 29 remaining churches today, we will learn that the message of the stave churches is still alive.

THE MIDDLE AGES AND THE FOREST

Encounters with stave churches inspire the atmosphere of a Norway existing eight to nine

The pilgrim and the bishop. Apparel from the 1100–1200s. (Hansen's **Våre klær gjennom tidene**)
Left: The stave church in its natural setting. Hopperstad, Vik in Sogn.

centuries ago. In their dark, tarred timbers, pointed gables, archways and dragon heads, gothic mysticism merges with visions of the forest.

The worshipper was immediately struck by an aura of mysticism as soon as he entered the church. He was confronted by an obtrusive darkness, only slightly alleviated by the shafts of light entering through small circular openings under the roof. Slowly the dimness receded and the interior emerged from the

darkness. First he sees the distant chancel and the altar, often in front of a semi-circular wall (apse). This wall might have been covered with paintings depicting the Last Supper and scenes from the life of Christ. Combined with the glowing tapers on the altar, the chancel appeared as a reflection of a heavenly play of colour and when entering the church, this was the first visual impression.

The worshippers themselves were a part of this atmosphere. Most of them were clad in woolen shifts belted with a cord at the waist, some also with the traditional garb of pilgrims on their way to Nidaros, a hooded cape and a stave. There were not many colourful red and blue capes of linen, but there were a few. These capes might have been lined with fur, but most of the congregation kept warm under shawls of sheepskin. The priest however, like the frescoed chancel and sacred vessels, was a lustrous sight in his glittering silken vestments.

An intense odour of wood and tar, wool and fur blended with the incense and wafted upwards to the roof beams. This

crown of shadowy, interlaced beams was like a dark and distant Nordic sky, brushed with a glow of "stars" entering through the high portholes of light. The church's interior ring of naked columns gave the feeling of being deep in the forest, complete with upright trees and spreading branches.

This shadowed, confined atmosphere bore the distinctive character of the North where bright sunshine was no more than an exception during a few hectic summer months. From the exterior the form of a tree is reflected in the roof's shingling, resembling a pine-cone, as well as in the general profile of the church. Theodor Kittelsen, a Norwegian artist, sees a picture of the mighty spruce in the stave churches' many-tiered progression to the heavens.

WITHSTANDING CENTURIES

Like the Viking ships, the stave churches represent an optimal use of the technique of building with wood. Their intricate system of columns and precise structural details unite to create an exacting stave construction

Top: Entering the church, the chancel and altar, "the tabernacle of Christ," are in one's direct line of vision. The Gol stave church.
Bottom: The stave church envisioned as a "forest grotto" with trees, branches and the "darkness of night".
Left: The stave church and the spruce forest. (Theodor Kittelsen, **The Ancient Church***)*

that has resisted the wear and tear of centuries. Two special conditions have made this possible. The first can be credited to a low wall of flat stones which raises the building above ground level. Originally, the staves and wall planks were embedded directly into the soil. One can imagine how well they lasted! The second condition was the way the columns, planks and supports were joined. They were dovetailed, pegged and wedged, never nailed or glued. Thus, the structure was completely flexible, and each joint could expand or contract depending upon damp or dry weather.

The following describes a stave church weathering a storm:

"In the Afternoon the Weather changed, and suddenly an entire Storm raged outside. It creaked in the old Church Walls, as if they were going to fall apart, it was as if each and every plank in the Stave construction would slide out of its Placement, break its very framework of Masts and Sills and bury everything beneath the vacillating Columns ... but little by little the raging wind blew more fitfully, became constant ... although the Storm increased rather than declined, soon no sound was to be heard in the Church Walls, wherein the entire Structure had settled and was now steeled and strengthened in the midst of the Storm." (Lorentz Dietrichson)

Section by section, the church rose from the framework of stones. The raft beams were placed first, intersecting one another at the corners and continuing outward to support any adjacent galleries or transepts. The tall staves which framed the nave were inserted into the mortised raft beams and joined on the top by a new square section of beams. This section supported the sharply pitched triangular roof trusses. In turn, these supported the expanse of the roof and the crowning bell tower which straddled the ridge of the roof on its four "legs". One might think that the building process would be complete, once the floor boards were installed and the protective wooden walls between the staves were put into place. But no, with the first gust of wind, a wooden tower like this would waver, twist and collapse onto the congregation.

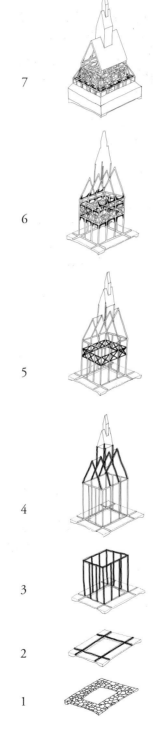

7

6

5

4

3

2

1

To be able to remain standing, the church needed additional support. This was done in three ways. The first was with a continuous "belt" of cross braces following the periphery of the room. Another way was by arches inserted between the staves in the form of curved wooden brackets. But even these measures were not sufficient. The low aisle section resting on the raft beams protruding from the nave was very critical to the structural support of the church. The aisles' steeply pitched roofs provided exterior support to the masts.

THE KINGDOM OF GOD ON EARTH

The stave church was God's House, a place for prayer and sacred worship. We see this in the church's location, its vertical symmetry, room proportions and ornamentation.

A stave church could not be built just anywhere. It demanded a high and open location, one that nature itself had prepared, conspicuous and prominent. Churches were to be placed on locations bearing the special imprint of God the Creator, on a peninsula, overlooking a fjord, at the turn of a river.

The church's vertical lines accentuated the choiceness of these locations. Verticality joined the structure to the heavens, and drew the church nave upwards past bare columns, sharp gables and soaring spires. Even the plaited pattern of the roof trusses lifted the line of sight upward.

This roof, with the frame of columns beneath it, might also be thought of as a baldachin. Ever since Antiquity, the baldachin's graphic illustration of the relation between heaven and earth has clearly signified a place of holiness. In this sense the baldachin's form becomes a dramatization of a congregation in prayer, a meeting between the human and the divine.

Inside the church, the cornerposts are essential. They are often accentuated, and are heavier and more richly decorated than the other structural elements. "They represent the four gospels whose teachings are the supporting foundation of all Christianity" is the description given in a sermon in the thirteenth century. This sermon was held during a church consecra-

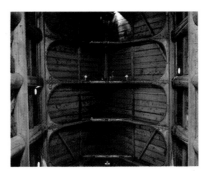

Top: The roof as a celestial baldachin. The Gol church, Norwegian Folk Museum, Oslo.
Bottom: The floor symbolizes the "humble men who bow in honour". (**Book of Sermons, 1200s**).
Left: Construction of a stave church, showing structural measures to prevent twisting and collapsing:
1 Stone foundation. 2 Sill beams.
3 Staves (posts) and upper beams .
4 Roof trusses and turret. 5 "Belt" of cross braces (St. Andrew's crosses).
6 Quadrant brackets between staves.
7 Quadrant brackets and aisle roof around stave construction.

tion, in which each section of the stave church's structure was related to spiritual values. The beams upon which the columns rest "signify God's apostles, the foundation of all Christianity". The floor boards represent "the humble men who bow in honour; the more they are exposed to the trampling feet of the congregation, the more support they provide".

The roof surface which protects the church from snow and inclement weather "represents the men ... whose prayers protect Christianity from temptation". This symbolic visualization of the spiritual forms of the stave church is seen clearly in a comparison with the early log houses and storehouses. The log house was built of horizontal logs, with massive tightly-joined walls enclosing a central open hearth directly beneath a smoke vent in the roof. The storehouse is formed like a log-built tower, raised from the ground, and with an exterior gallery under the outer edges of the roof. Indeed their formation is inspired by different sources. The stave church reflected Romanesque and Gothic cathedral architectu-

re, while the storehouse was a remnant of the defense towers of a fortress, and the log house originated in the steppes of Russia.

Most important however, is how each of these structures reveals its special function. The heaviness of a log house expresses the protection of its inhabitants from extreme weather conditions, and the storehouse, raised well above ground, represents the safekeeping of the harvest and food. The angle of their roofs is also important. While the stave church's gables are sharp and dynamic, the gables' angles on the log house and storehouse are broad and blunt, resulting in the houses lying low in the terrain beneath heavy grass roofs. The graceful and ascending represent a spiritual longing, the heavy and anchored, earthly pursuits.

The use of space in the stave church also reflects ancient interpretations of God's kingdom on earth. The earliest churches consisted of a simple, square room with a small chancel placed at one end. The chancel held the altar and the burning tapers; the nave held the kneeling congregation.

Top: Smoke ventilation in a log house. The Åmlid house at the Norwegian Folk Museum, Oslo.
Bottom: The storage house rising from its pillars. Kleivi, Telemark.
Left: The roof symbolizes the "men whose prayers protect Christianity from temptation". (**Book of Sermons**)

Therefore their symbolism varied, or, as written in the *Book of Sermons,* "the chancel, or choir, stand for the holy men in heaven, and the nave, Christian men on earth". Both the rectangular church and the cruciform church had similar symbolic significance. The first, with columns on either side from the entrance to the chancel, has roots that go back to the first Christian basilicas. The central room forms a passage, a "Via Sacra" depicting the life of a Christian, starting at the entrance and continuing forward to death in Christ at the altar. The cruciform church, the central church may have had eastern Byzantine roots, perhaps from the time that Sigurd Jorsalfar journeyed to Constantinople. The cruciform church speaks for itself: the congregation literally settled into a room that signified Christ.

The pentices that surrounded the inner church room also had many interpretations. Travellers from afar received protection from rain and snow while waiting for the church service, and we know that the unbaptized followed the church service from the galleries through small holes in the walls. From time immemorial circling something one wanted to own has been a significant action. We know that the Nordic rules for transferrals of land ownership required the purchaser to walk around the boundaries of his newly-acquired fields before his ownership was official. The cloister's ambulatories around the altar of a gothic

cathedral provided a similar opportunity for the flow of pilgrims.

The ambulatory satisfied man's longing to be near the sacred in the same way as the church's pentices did in a newly converted Norway. The dragon heads with their outstretched tongues, sneered from the gable edges as graphic representations of evil paying lip service to the good. Ancient heathen motifs, following the era of migration and coming from Irish and Germanic sources, symbolized the destructive forces which were now neutralized and bound to the temple of the "White Christ". These pagan motifs snapped aggressively at their foes, for they knew that no one understood the wiles of evil better than those who had formerly been members of the same team.

This struggle is concentrated around the main entrance to the church, which in its exalted form represented "the true faith which leads us to universal Christianity" *(Book of Sermons)*. The entrance is so narrow that only one person can enter at a time; the sacred was to be approached alone, without the company of evil. At the opening, one is

Top: The mysticism of the nave; "Via Sacra" – a motif from early Christian basilicas. Santa Maria in Cosmedin, Rome, founded 6th century.
Left: The pentice, a place for waiting, processions, and protection. Hopperstad church, Vik in Sogn.

encircled by a richly-carved frenzy of struggling serpents, dragons and lions. Here, the fabled animals of the Vikings are juxtaposed with Christian portrayals of the battle between good and evil. The struggle is particularly extreme here at the entrance to the sanctuary, the threshold to salvation.

A HUMAN MONUMENT

Stave churches are national monuments.

They bear witness to a time

of change, a time when Norway, like the rest of Europe, sought consolidation and unity after the chaos of mass migrations.

In 1015 A.D., a young man stepped ashore in Norway after many years as a Viking on the continent. This youth, Olaf Haraldsson, wanted to unite Norway under the rule of one king, and to form a national government on the European model. While away from Norway, Olav had converted to Christianity. With missionary zeal, he charged throughout his homeland bearing the banner of the Cross. With strong resistance, the Norwegian people converted to Christianity. The stave churches bear witness to this.

The churches also show another side of history, how architecture can herald human values. They tell of building with wisdom and forethought in consideration of extreme weather conditions, of building beautifully in harmony with the terrain, with natural materials. But perhaps most importantly, stave churches bear witness to the human need for an aura of light in a world that will always be inhabited by wild dragons.

BORGUND
STAVE CHURCH

LÆRDAL IN SOGN

NO ONE KNOWS how much of his sermon the priest had given when the shot that killed the reindeer went off. Nor does anyone know who shot the animal, nor why, of all times, it happened during a church service. History has been silent about most of this story, but we do know that a stuffed reindeer was on display in the Borgund stave church in 1688. This reindeer had been shot while a church service was in progress. It is up to our own imagination: could the poor animal have strayed in through an open door and disturbed the priest and his congregation? Could the reindeer have distracted a person in the church who had seen it through a window (post-Reformation churches had windows) and without giving a thought to the priest or the Divine Word had this church-goer simply rushed out before the animal could escape? Another dilemma is why had the reindeer been stuffed and displayed in the church? Well, 200 years have passed, and whatever the deer represented, hunting trophy or sacred symbol, it was removed from the church a long time ago.

The Borgund stave church stands like a crown jewel in the narrow valley at the head of the Sognefjord, surrounded by lush vegetation and craggy mountains. The Danish poet Holger Drachmann described the church in 1886:

"... a whim of childlike brilliance, a house for beetles, whittled from a naive giant's playful knife, with modest crosses and large-nosed dragons, wrinkled and gnarled, twig upon twig. The interior is like a smokehouse dedicated to a mystic cult in which the darkness of the sagas overwhelms the faintly smouldering tapers of Catholicism, which cast their light on farmers' iron-clad axes and the flowing beards of Viking Kings – in all honesty, a disagreeable experience."

The Borgund stave church, which is dedicated to St. Andrew, is mentioned for the first time in *Bjorgynjar Kalfskinn,* a register of churches in the Bergen diocese from about 1360, although it is likely that it was built in the last decades of the 12th century. Borgund is the best preserved of our 29 stave churches, and has served as a model for many church restorations such as the Gol and Hopperstad chur-

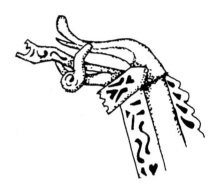

The Borgund stave church lies in the narrow valley that stretches from Lærdal, at the end of the Sognefjord, up to Fillefjell.

17

ches and the Fantoft stave church in Bergen, which has since burned down. The Borgund stave church could have also become the victim of flames in 1782, when a mentally disturbed woman set fire to it. As luck would have it, a local person was passing by the church just then, and managed to call for help.

The church has three naves, a chancel and an apse. A Romanesque gallery with carved portals facing west and south, surrounds the entire structure. The west portal is especially richly decorated in the contemporary carving style: battling dragon-like animals entwined in rhythmic vine motifs.

View toward the chancel.

The quantity of roofs, gables, spires and dragon heads, reminiscent of the Baroque style, are in strong contrast to the simplicity of the interior. The interior is dominated by posts which support the high main roof and separate the room into a rectangular central section and the narrow and lower-ceilinged area along the outer walls.

The church interior is modestly ornamented and practically in total darkness. A leaflet prepared by the Society for the Preservation of Norwegian Ancient Monuments in 1898 gives the following excellent description:

"If the doors are closed, we are surprised to find ourselves in almost total darkness, a darkness which is magnified by small strips of light that occasionally force their way from the original window in the west gable or from the small peep-holes along the top of the longitudinal walls. Experiencing this, one must recall that the religious service consisted of a short service at the altar by candlelight. There was actually no need to illuminate the congregation's area since psalm books were not in use then."

The altar, graced with sacred vessels of gilded silver or copper glowing from the light of candelabras and wrought-iron torches, must have been a powerful and dramatic contrast to the dark church. The priest and his sermon must have commanded the full attention of the congregation, which stood during the service – a bench or raised floor section along the wall was meant for the elderly or the infirm.

Today there is nothing left of the original inventory – the altarpiece and pulpit date from after the Reformation. But there are many runic inscriptions on the inner and outer walls which linguists can place in the 1100s. One of these, "God help each person who helps my journey", may refer to a desire to set out on a pilgrimage, perhaps northward to the reliquary of St. Olav in the Nidaros Cathedral in Trondheim? The ancient roadway, cut into the hillside by the graveyard, is thought to be the one used in the Middle Ages, the one taken by King Sverre and his men when they were travelling through the valley.

URNES
STAVE CHURCH

LUSTER IN SOGN

THE BELLS HAVE been rung for vespers. The parish is gathered in the stave church in Ornes (Urnes) to pray for victory over their enemy and for the Lord's protection of father, son, brother and friend. Further out in the fjord, at Fimreite, the battle between King Sverre's "Birkebeiner" and King Magnus Erlingsson's "Heklunger", is being waged in full. Many a brave member of the parish has joined the battle on the side of King Magnus Erlingsson, including Jon and Munan Gautsson, sons of the nobleman Gautr of Ornes.

But King Sverre is the victor. As the sun sets, the King stands on the deck of his ship, "Mariasuden", intoning a "Kyrie Eleison" in thanksgiving to the Saviour. King Magnus has fallen, taking with him most of the nobility south of Trøndelag.

The date is the 15th of June, St. Vitus' Day in the year of the Lord 1184.

The Urnes stave church, Queen of the stave churches, rises from a height of 120 metres above the sea, and has a beautiful view inward toward Luster and outward over the Sognefjord. "Her Majesty" receives from the sea – since access to this church is possible by boat. People have approached this church by rowboat or under sail ever since the end of the Viking Age, to gather in prayer to the Christian God, "Hvitekrist". Important sections of the Urnes stave church, probably the oldest of its type, were originally in an even older place of worship on the same site. In 1956–57, during excavations beneath the church, architect Håkon Christie found traces of post holes for an older and smaller church. The oldest decorations in the Urnes church, including the main portal and two gable sections, were originally from this church, or from one that was even older. The unique ornamentation in the Urnes church has become known as the "Urnes style".

The Urnes style has been called "the swan song of pagan animal-patterned ornamentation". However, although this ornamentation belongs to the final style of the Viking Period, it was not necessarily from pagan times. The same motifs have been found in Uppland, on a number of Swedish runic stones dating from about 1060. At that time, even the most remote areas had been converted to Christianity.

FACTS

Single-nave church with 16 columns, built 1130–1150.
Richly carved post capitals in Anglo-Norman style with figures in faint relief.
1100s: Calvary group with Christ, Mary and John the Baptist, bishop's chair in chancel.
Lighting in the form of a wrought iron viking ship, two candlesticks with inlaid enamel-work from Limoges, probably from the Middle Ages.
1600s: Carved pulpit, pentice and rood screen.
1601: Chancel extended.
1659: Pulpit.
1699: Altar-piece.
1700: Gallery.
1704: Bell turret.
1902: Restoration supervised by J.Z.M. Kielland.
1956–1957: Excavations by building contractor O.H. Stadskleiv and architect Kristian Bjerknes.

The opulent carvings in the "Urnes style" on the panels of the north portal as well as the north wall are from an older church on this site. The church is owned by the Society for the Preservation of Ancient Norwegian Monuments. It is sometimes used during summer.

The Urnes carvings are not influenced by the earliest Romanesque Christian art style, which had begun to appear in places such as Ringerike, (the "Ringerike style") in which flower and leaf ornamentation gradually replaced animal ornamentation. The Urnes style's characteristic quadrupeds and delicacy of line, with animals coiled around each other, entwined in broad and narrow bands, is clearly the work of a master craftsman. This style was so vital that traces of it are clearly visible far into the Gothic period of architecture.

The interior of the Urnes church is clearly marked by post-Reformation alterations, although the church interior's medieval form is still intact. The carved capitals on the staves in the intricate central section of the nave are particularly interesting. A crucifix above the chancel arch from the early Middle Ages depicts Christ in a customary medieval representation, a triumphant king bearing a crown. From the church's medieval inventory, two extremely unusual and beautiful metal and enamel candlesticks from the 1200s deserve particular note. They actually come from Limoges. One can only speculate as to how they arrived at this remote mountain community in Norway in those days.

There are many legends associated with the Urnes stave church, including a variation of the folk saga "Bendik and Årolilja" which is in turn based on the Danish saga about Hagbard and Signe. According to tradition, Habor (Hagbard) and Signe's tragic love story took place at Urnes. In earlier times, people could even point to where the gallows had been when Habor was hanged, and where the cage in which the grieving Signe lived and eventually took her own life.

Detail from the northern portal which probably dates from an earlier church at Urnes. This is a typical example of the "Urnes style".

"The Queen of stave churches" has a magnificent setting on the steep promontory, Urneset, 120 metres above sea level.

(Left) No wonder the Urnes stave church is on UNESCO's World Heritage List.

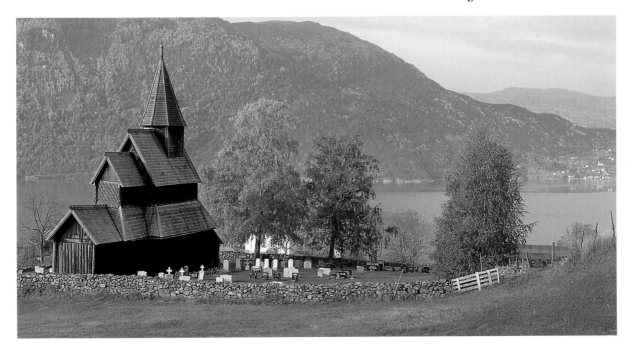

KAUPANGER
STAVE CHURCH

SOGN

CHRISTMAS WAS CELEBRATED in an unusual way in Kaupanger in the year of the Lord, 1183. These were troubled times. Sverre Sigurdsson, who was at war with Magnus Erlingsson to win absolute power over Norway, had recently conquered West Norway and appointed new governors in Rogaland and Hordaland. However, Magnus still had many followers and the people of Sogn were among those who looked askance upon Sverre's appointments. Their displeasure was not lessened when Sverre's governors, who had decided to celebrate Christmas in Lusekaupangen, demanded "juleveitsle", free room and board for themselves and their men. The people of Sogn and Eid banded together and journeyed to Kaupanger, where many other men joined their group. It was Christmas Eve, and they attacked King Sverre's governors.

Perhaps Arngeir, vicar of the little stave church in Kaupanger was in his pulpit proclaiming the joyous message of Christmas when the battle was at its worst. The vicar's sons, Gaut and Karlshovud, were among the leaders of the battle.

"Glory to God in the highest, and on earth peace, good will toward men ..."

The people of Sogn claimed justifiable rage and the few persons among the governors' men who managed to escape "took the road by land northward to King Sverre (he was then in Trondheim) and reported what had happened, telling that the people of Sogn had said that they had only killed thieves and robbers, persons they could not be fined for killing".

King Sverre responded quickly. He sent his men to Lusekaupangen the following summer and they "ravaged everything they could find of value and set fire to the trading center". Shortly after this, at the Battle of Fimreite, Magnus Erlingsson was killed.

Was the stave church in Kaupanger also destroyed by fire in the summer of 1184? Sverre's saga does not mention the church. King Sverre's men were ordered to spare the churches, but there is reason to believe that this church fell prey to the flames. Archaeological excavations have found traces of a fire layer, confirming that two stave

F A C T S

Masted stave church, probably from the last decade of the 1100s, built on the same toft as two older stave churches with earthed post holes. Expanded and lengthened in the Middle Ages.
Ca 1600–1650: Church acquires new windows in the nave and chancel, a pulpit, altar-piece, and memorial plaques. Painted wall decorations.
1862: Rebuilt to an open, light church in the style of the 19th century. Windows from 17th century covered over and replaced with 51 new windows. New vestibule erected.
1965: The church's 17th century atmosphere recreated, partly on the basis of archaeological finds, partly through comparison with other unaltered 17th century buildings. The church exterior covered with horizontal panelling and painted grey/brown. Restoration by architect Kristian Bjerknes.
The Kaupanger stave church has been used almost continuously and is still the local parish church.

The chancel and its altar-piece from 1634, showing the crucified Christ, Mary and St. John the Baptist. To the left, and from the same period, the font with its domed, hexagonal cover.

churches had been on this site previously, both with earthed post holes. The finds also revealed that the eldest of the three churches, which was built in the second half of the 1100s, had been torn down even though it was in good condition. It may have simply become too small, since the church that replaced it, which was destroyed by fire some time in the late 1100s, was a good deal larger. The present church, the largest stave church in the Sogn area, measured 10.25 m by 7.5 m when it was built, but this one must have also become too small. Sometime between 1200 and 1350 it was extended by 3.5 meters.

The size of the church may have been a result of the area's importance as a center of trade. The old Norse word "kaupangr" means trading post or marketplace.

The exterior of the Kaupanger stave church as it is today is a definite reflection of 17th century architecture, when its bell turrets, vestibule, and windows were added, and the outer walls were panelled. Elements from the 16th century have also left their mark in the church inventory, such as the pulpit, altar-piece, memorial plaques and painted decorations, but they are barely noticed when experiencing the extended interior's forest of slender columns. There are eight columns on each of the long sides which present a perfect illustration of the term "masted basilica".

Kaupanger is the largest of Sogn's stave churches. Seventeenth century exterior.

HOPPERSTAD
STAVE CHURCH

VIK IN SOGN

THE YEAR 1875 was a turning point in the history of the community. There was a new church. No longer was it necessary for toes to be curled inside footwear because of chilly drafts creeping along the floorboards, and even in mid-winter, gloveless hands could fold themselves around psalm books. And "Father" could preach from his pulpit with renewed hope that the Word would penetrate the thirsty souls of the congregation.

The former place of worship, the Hopperstad stave church, had played out its role long ago. The parish paid little attention to their old church's state of deterioration, although a few persons must have been aware of recent efforts to preserve stave churches as relics of the past. Most likely, the Society for the Preservation of Norwegian Ancient Monuments, which was founded in 1844, was the driving force behind these efforts. Nevertheless, there was a majority vote to demolish the church.

Fortunately, architect Peter Blix was the right person in the right place at the right time. He put a halt to the demolition of the church, and in 1882 it was sold "lock stock and barrel" to the Society for the Preservation of Norwegian Ancient Monuments.

Blix deserves credit for his fine restoration of this church, a restoration which was said to "comply totally with the popular idea of a stave church, with exterior galleries, numerous steep roof angles and a small tower astride the ridgetop". This was not a simple task. Not only was the church in disrepair, its exterior and interior had been rebuilt and "renewed" over the years, and completely covered by horizontal panelling. In other words, the church was far from the medieval church we admire today. Blix had asked himself the obvious question: What did the church look like when it was built in the last decades of the 1100s? He found the answer in another church, the Borgund stave church, which was from the same era and the best preserved of all of Norway's stave churches. After six years of work, the exterior gallery, the ridge turrets and steeple, the apse with tower and spire and exterior shingling were in place, all modelled after the Borgund stave church.

The intention underlying the construction of both churches has

FACTS

Triple-naved stave church with 16 posts, built 1130.
1300–1350: Baldachin.
1650–1700: Painted wall decorations.
1621: Renaissance altar-piece.
1884: Ownership of church assumed by the Society for the Preservation of Norwegian Ancient Monuments.
1885–1891: Church restored to its original medieval style (patterned on the Borgund stave church) by architect Peter Blix.
The church is only used on Midsummer's Eve.

clearly been the same, to re-create a columned basilica in wood. Both churches have 16 masts with cube-shaped capitals, and the placement of these masts in the chancels and naves of both churches is similar. In addition, all of the interior construction is practically identical. But while the central section of the Urnes church is richly ornamented, the interior of Hopperstad is almost devoid of ornamentation. The church might have had painted wall decorations in the Middle Ages as among other finds, there are traces of painted pictures of saints on the chancel's two free-standing masts. When architect Blix appeared on the scene with his "rescue-squad", painted wall decorations from the 1600s were still intact. But Blix found these "recent" decorations totally without charm. Rigidly adhering to his preference for a puristic medieval style, he ruthlessly removed the Baroque innovations.

When entering the bare central section of the church, the almost austere Renaissance-style panels in the chancel and main altar are directly in one's line of sight. But attention is drawn quickly to one of the two side altars at the chancel entrance, toward an unusual canopy, a baldachin. This is Scandinavia's finest example of an original baldachin. It is attached to the interior columns on three sides, while its fourth side is supported by a free-standing post. The baldachin, an architectural rarity, is probably from the first half of the 14th century. Its elaborately carved exterior includes four carved heads representing Christ, a king, a queen and a munk. Eight circular sections on the ceiling of the baldachin are painted with scenes from the life of the Virgin Mary, and Latin inscriptions.

Hopperstad was restored in the late 1800s, modelled after the Borgund stave church.

UNDREDAL
STAVE CHURCH

SOGN

"They rowed the fjord
they crossed the beach
they rode the hills
they waded over the bay ..."

PEOPLE HAVE BEEN going to services in the Undredal stave church for hundreds of years, just as Aslaug Vaa's poem describes. And this is how people still come to this little white church. It is nestled in the heart of a small community (population in 1987, ca. 100) on the Aurlandsfjord and enjoys an incredible view, surveying the sea, the undulating hills of green, and the snow-capped mountains.

Undredal is one of Norway's oldest stave churches and may have been built or even used as early as 1147, a date found on a roof truss during recent repair work. The first recorded mention of this church is in a letter from Bishop Audfinn in Bjørgvin in 1321, appointing Pål Bårdson as the priest at Undrudal Kapella (or Undru Kapella). Pål Bårdson eventually became King Magnus' chancellor and was later the Archbishop of Nidaros. Also, a document from Avignon in 1348 relates that Pope Clemens VI granted Canon Odd Ogmundsson the curacy of the St. Nicholas Chapel in Undredal.

This church, like the Eidsborg stave church, was also dedicated to St. Nicholas. It was one of seven or eight churches (3–4 may have been privately owned) in the district before the arrival of the bubonic plague. After this devastating plague, only two churches remained, and one of them was Undredal. Not even the "Black Death" of our modern times, emigration to urban areas, has turned this church into a museum piece. It is still in use – although seating only about 40 persons, it is probably the smallest in Scandinavia – and shares a pastor with the other parishes in the area.

Bookkeeping accounts from the 17th and 18th centuries bear witness to the fact that financing this little church has often been troublesome. The church received "land rent" from many farms, property taxes which were paid in kind. Translated into money, this amounted to about 7 riksdaler (silver coins) in 1670. In that same year, church expenses were 19 riksdaler, of which 13 were owed to the vicar. In

FACTS

Single-nave stave church, possibly built in the mid-1100s.
Pentice mentioned in 1665 but no traces of this have been found.
Marks in the wall show that the church once had a gallery in the nave, and later, also in the western annex (the latter until the 1860s).
Probably from the Middle Ages: Chandelier with five carved stags' heads.
1647: Kneeler.
1696: Pulpit.
1600s: Walls and ceiling receive painted decorations.
1722: Major reconstruction of church.
1962: Church restored. Three layers of paint removed to bring forth decorations on walls and ceiling. Beneath the oldest layer of paint, pictures including mythical animals as well as various symbolic marks were found.
The church is still in use.

The Undredal stave church has been in use ever since it was built in the mid-1100s.

1700, income was still less than expenses, but the church deficit of 10 riksdaler was the result of comprehensive repairs on the church. Thirteen years later, the difference between income and expenses had become considerably larger. Not only had the church fallen into debt on the home front. In 1713, for some unknown reason, Undredal and many other Norwegian churches had to pay out 2 marks (1 mark = ca 1/5 of a riksdaler) to a Lutheran school in London, and 4 marks to a school that had burned down in Altona, now a suburb of Hamburg, then a Danish territory!

In 1722 the Undredal stave church underwent a major reconstruction, the results of which can be seen in the present church. Its medieval stave construction and subsequent ornamentation such as the 17th century vines and "star-sown" barrel-vaulted ceiling, create a harmonious effect.

And when the sexton appears in the centre of the church and "rings out" the congregation after the service, Undredal being one of the few churches in Norway that still maintains this tradition, one is confronted with a deep feeling of continuity:

Seating only 40, Undredal is probably Scandinavia's smallest church that is still in use.

"From the south and the north
all shook hands
– Then rowed the fjord –
and crossed the beach –"

RØLDAL
STAVE CHURCH

RØLDAL

"In the church at Røldal a picture was placed
for the salvation of many a glad soul,
the sick and infirm to this spot traced
and returned with their health made whole."

A.O. VINJE: "Storegut"

The drinking bouts, where the beer was blessed in the Names of the Saviour and the Blessed Virgin, had come to an end. The newly-sprouted birch branches hanging in houses, stables, cowsheds and pens for protection from evil spirits, were wilting, and down by the lake, Røldalsvatnet, the bonfire had dwindled to a few glowing cinders. It was night-time. But the small tarred church at the northern end of the lake was crowded. People from far and wide had come for midnight mass, many of them suffering from physical ailments, but strongly believing that the Saviour would once again perform miracles on this Midsummer's Eve, *Jonsoknatt*. The crucifix in this church had an extraordinary aspect: every year, on Midsummer's Eve, beads of sweat formed on the brow of the figure. And those who rubbed this moisture over their infirmities were cured.

The mass is in progress. Finally the moment everyone is waiting for has arrived. The priest and his assistant remove the crucifix from the chancel arch and place it on the altar. While singing psalms, the sick, paralysed, lame and blind, are helped to the altar, one at a time. They touch a linen cloth to the brow of the Christ figure and stroke the cloth over their infirmities. Or they hide the cloth next to their bodies. Some are here to fetch a sacred cloth for a person who is too ill to make the journey.

After the Reformation in 1536, the newly-appointed clergy looked upon such sinful "Papist practice" with distaste. During an official visit to Vinje in 1622, Oslo Bishop Nils Glostrup wrote that he had heard of "grave Idolatry in Relledalen" which he intended to combat with "effective Measures".

The custom of presenting the church with gifts to ensure the Lord's favour was deeply ingrained. As recently as 1704, the Hjelmeland congregation donated a silver case for altar bread to the

F A C T S

A single-nave church with masts inserted along the longitudinal walls.
Built in the 13th century.
Crucifix from about 1250.
Soapstone font from the 13th century.
The chancel arch altered and church interior decorated with floral paintings, "rosepainting", in the 17th century.
1627: Renaissance-style pulpit erected.
1629: Altar-piece painted by Gotfrid Hendtzchell.
1844: Church is repaired, including installation of a flat ceiling; the nave is extended to the west and a tower is erected.
1918: Restoration completed under the direction of architect Jens Z. Kielland. The partially preserved 17th-century wall decorations in the chancel and nave restored by Domenico Erdmann. A narrower square-ended chancel is added by architect Kielland.
The stave church is still the main church of the parish.

church. The case was inscribed with a plea for help from the wolf who was killing their livestock:

Church interior, with the miraculous crucifix and rose-painted walls.

"... Protect cattle and sheep, release them from warring with wolves."

And whatever "effective Measures" the church used to prevent worship of the crucifix, annual pilgrimages and secret midnight masses for the infirm in the Røldal church continued until 1835, when these "idolatrous vigils" were finally brought to a stop.

Numerous crosses carved into the outer walls of the church bear witness to centuries of pilgrimages. But whether miracles really happened here is uncertain. Subsequent, more rational eras have tried to find circumstantial explanations for the phenomenon. One theory is that the beads of sweat secreted by the figure were nothing more than condensation caused by the combination of crowds of people and numerous burning candles. And *if* there were one or two cures, they may have inspired Hans Christian Anderson's timeless story about the famous feather that became five hens.

Regardless of what really happened, the miraculous crucifix in Røldal will remain in our thoughts. And when you are inside this beautifully ornamented medieval church, looking at the suffering Christ figure hanging over the chancel arch, a very strange feeling will come over you. No one knows ...

It used to be difficult to get to the remote Røldalkyrkja. Nevertheless it became a destination for pilgrims because of its crucifix which allegedly performed miracles.

HEDDAL
STAVE CHURCH

TELEMARK

ONCE UPON A TIME, a church was built by a troll. The church was called *Ryginar* and was in a place called Heitradali, in Telemark. This place of worship was so large and so grand that it could not possibly have been the work of a human being – it was rumoured that sorcery must have been involved. And this is the legend:

When Christianity came to this land, many farmers wished to raise a church in the honour of the new Christian God, "Hvitekrist". The name of one of the farmers was Raud Rygi. One day a stranger came to him and offered to build the church. But Raud Rygi would have to pay in one of three ways: Fetch the sun and the moon from the heavens, pierce his heart and let the blood flow, or find out the name of the stranger. Raud Rygi thought these conditions were fair enough, but the stranger was a fearfully efficient builder and Raud soon understood that the church would be finished in three days. This made him fear for his life. As he paced in his fields, wondering what to do, he heard a clear, beautiful lullaby from the depths of Svintryberget, the mountain southeast of the church.

> Hush, hush my little one
> Finn will bring the moon tomorrow,
> saving neither christian heart nor sun
> to keep his child from sorrow.

Then Raud understood that the stranger was a mountain troll and that his name was Finn. On the third day, Finn arrived and offered the completed church to Raud. When they went into the church, Raud hit the main post in the centre of the church and said, "This is crooked, Finn". "It can be even crookeder," answered Finn, and raced from the church to his mountain abode in Himingfjell (Lifjell).

Although more rational explanations for the church's existence turned up later, wonderment about this impressive piece of architecture, our largest stave church, has not lessened over the years. For example, Bishop Jens Nilssøn wrote the following about the church after having seen it on an official visit in 1595:

"Heiterdal's church is a wooden structure, built in a most amazing

FACTS

Masted stave church with a 20-masted main nave, chancel with 6 free masts, apse, 2 transepts, 3 towers and pentice, built ca 1250. The chancel is most likely a section of the nave from an older church from the 1100s. The main nave and the chancel's apse added about 100 years later.
1200s: Painted antemensale from the main altar, now at the University Museum of National Antiquities.
1100–1200: Carved church bench, now in the Gol stave church, at Bygdøy's Norwegian Folk Museum in Oslo.
Middle Ages: Carved chair.
1600s: Flat ceiling installed, painted decoration.
1667: Altar-piece.
1848–1851: Restoration by Danish architect Johan Henrik Nebelong.
1952–1954: Reconstruction to church's original medieval appearance by architects Gudolf Blakstad and Herman Munthe-Kaas.
The church is still in use.

Roof upon roof, tower upon tower. Heddal, which is called "a gothic cathedral in wood", is Norway's largest stave church.

manner with three small towers, one on the eastern end of the chancel, one on the centre of the chancel, and one, the largest, with bells hanging from it, on the centre of the church."

"Our most luxurious and beautiful monument of this kind," was art historian and professor Lorentz Dietrichson's description of the church. Unlike so many other churches, Heddal is not placed on a high elevation, but on the level field along the Heddøla River. This made it easy for the farmers who lived around Lake Heddal, to get themselves to church by boat.

Section from one of the entrances.

It is likely that this church, referred to as "a gothic cathedral in wood," and consecrated to the Virgin Mary, was built in about 1250 during the prosperous reign of Håkon Håkonsson. This date is deduced from a runic inscription on the fourth wall board to the right of the southern entrance portal, and from carvings on the portal itself in which foliage and vine ornamentation make a strong appearance in combination with the older animal ornamentation. However there is no recorded mention of the church until 1315, in connection with a change of ownership. Like many other churches, the Heddal stave church is possibly the second on the same location. It is thought that the chancel of the present structure was originally the nave of a smaller church from the 1100s.

The Heddal church did not escape post-Reformation fervour either. In the mid-1600s, its high central section was replaced with a low, flat ceiling, and windows were fitted in just below the ceiling. The interior remained unchanged until ca 1850, and it was immortalized in the paintings of two of Norway's greatest National Romanticists, Adolph Tidemand and Johannes Flintoe. But then came the Danish architect, Johan Henrik Nebelong, whose restoration destroyed the 17th century interior. This should never have been permitted, even his contemporaries shunned the new interior. Painter J.C. Dahl, the first to recognize the cultural value of our stave churches, maintained that Heddal had become a "Wedding Cake Temple". Nevertheless, 100 years passed before director H.B. Holta at the Tinfoss industrial complex offered to pay for the restoration of the church "back" to its original medieval appearance. Architects Gudolf Blakstad and Herman Munthe-Kaas managed to reconstruct the main architectural elements of the interior and to bring forth the surviving decoration from the Middle Ages and the 1600s.

The spacious dimensions of the Heddal stave church (height 26 meters, length 20 meters) as well as its opulent inventory bear witness to a prosperous country and community. Much of the original inventory has been removed from the church. However the church still has many treasures such as a stave-built medieval chair in the chancel, and an altar-piece from 1667 depicting the Crucifixion and the Lord's Supper.

Chancel and its altar-piece from 1667.

EIDSBORG
STAVE CHURCH

LÅRDAL

WHERE SHOULD THE church be built? In spite of strongly differing opinions, a place called Kirkedalen was finally chosen. While the work progressed, local arguments continued to flourish. One evening, the craftsmen left their tools behind what was called "Church rock", and when they returned the next morning, their tools were gone. After an exhaustive search they were found – and the church now stands on this spot. Everyone agreed this had been a sign from the powers above, and peace finally came to the inhabitants of the valley.

New problems arose: How could they have a burial ground here in this rocky terrain? Two local girls who had been sentenced to death, possibly for infanticide, were given an unusual chance to save their lives. If they could collect enough soil for the church graveyard, they would be pardoned. But they had to carry the soil in their skirts. The girls set to work, and of course, succeeded in their impossible task. Therefore, many of their fellow villagers were put to rest in the burial ground long before they were.

"... all a lie – a damnable tale?" Perhaps. But it is worth noting that the constitution of the soil in the churchyard is totally different from the other soil in the area.

This is the story of how the Eidsborg stave church was built in about 1250, one of the last to be built in Norway before the Black Death made its disastrous appearance in 1349.

Like most other stave churches, this one is also built with the district's towering heartwood pine. The single-nave church is surrounded by a solid-walled pentice to the south, west and north. From the exterior, the pentice looks large because of the extension of the nave and the addition of the chancel (with the same width as the nave) in the 1800s. Olav Bakken's *Lårdalssoga* from 1978 describes the church as "partially old and partially new".

The exterior of the church is distinctive. The roof, posts and walls are clad with shingles, with the exception of the west gable, which is clad in panels of imitation shingle.

The church appears smaller from the inside. The nave, almost a square, has a 7-meter roof truss and is only 30 square meters in area.

FACTS

Single-nave church built in about 1250.
1604 and 1609: Painted with acanthus ornamentation.
1826: Nave is extended by its width, in notched logs.
1845: A chancel is added, interior panelling and a flat ceiling are installed.
1927–1929: The church is restored to its medieval appearance by architect George Eliassen.
Ca 1980: Ornamentation in the extended nave executed by architect Arnstein Arneberg, based on a wall fragment from an earlier stave church in Lårdal.
The stave church is still the main church of the parish.

This stave church is on a small hill west of the lake, Eidsborgtjønni, and is dedicated to St. Nicholas of Bari.

On each of the four monumental corner posts, which have large bell-shaped bases, a man's name is carved in runic script.

"In runes are carved four men of fame
On, Grip, Gunnar and Asgeir were their names.
Each man raised a corner post on this site,
grandly turned columns borne with might."

This fantasy about the runes on the corner posts is initialled by "J.R." in an 1880 issue of the periodical "Fedraheimen".

The Eidsborg stave church was dedicated to St. Nicholas of Bari. Ever since the early Middle Ages, a painted wooden statue depicting St. Nicholas in religious robes has been in the church. He was "no larger than a small 12-year-old boy". Like the miraculous crucifix at the Røldal stave church, St. Nicholas won fame because of a ceremony on Midsummer Night's Eve. On this evening, the statue was taken from the church and carried to a nearby lake, Eidsborgtjønni, and "bathed very ceremoniously". The statue was then carried three times around the lake before being returned to the church. The cleansing was to symbolize the redemption of sin, but there are some who maintain that it encouraged Nicholas to bless the farmers with productive crops.

The original statue of St. Nicholas was brought to the University Museum of National Antiquities in Oslo many years ago. The statue in the church is a copy.

The church is entirely clad with wooden shingles.

ROLLAG
STAVE CHURCH

NUMEDAL

WHILE THE FLESBERG and Nore stave churches were built in the flat-lands, Rollag's church, like Uvdal's was placed on the hillside with a spacious view of the valley and the River Lågen. Little is left of the medieval stave church at Rollag which is, like Flesberg, one of the oldest of Numedal's stave churches. All that remains are the four corner posts and some fragments in the transepts from the original nave. The transepts were built in the late 1600s when the ancient medieval church was literally "sinking into ruin", making way for the present Baroque church.

The original stave church was small and single-naved and had a stave-built chancel with apse and most likely, an exterior gallery surrounding the building. The church may have had a central mast like the churches in Nore and Uvdal.

It is understandable that the Rollag church's interior and exterior are similar to the three other stave churches in the area. Although these churches may have been quite different when they were built, they developed into fairly similar structures during the 17th and 18th centuries since their additions and alterations were taking place at about the same time. The same craftsmen and artists often travelled from church to church and of course, this too contributed to a certain standardization. For example, the decorations in Rollag's chancel are similar to those in Nore and Uvdal. The beautiful shade of blue that was applied to Rollag's interior in the mid-1700s is reminiscent of the work of the "painter of blue" who had decorated the Uvdal church a few decades earlier. Most likely, the same painter was at work in both churches.

Nevertheless, in spite of its colours and ornamentation, the central section of the church in Rollag presents a stiff and dignified atmosphere rather than an intimate one. As in so many other 17th century churches, there are signs of the Baroque principle that individual elements should be subordinate to the whole. There is an underlying tone of authority set by prestigious vicars from earlier centuries in the Rollag church. In Uvdal and Nore, memorial plaques and portraits of the clergy are only conspicuous by their absence. In these churches the little man's voice is heard through the floral painters' longing for

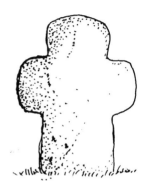

FACTS

Single-nave church, probably from the late Middle Ages. The medieval church had a stave-built chancel with an apse and most likely a pentice on all sides. Possibly a central mast.
A large stone cross is outside the church. This was found in a burial chamber beneath the chancel and is probably older than the church and used as a gathering place for the congregation in the "pioneer days" of Christianity.
1652 or 1653: Windows installed, walls decorated.
Ca 1660: Church modified and the chancel enlarged.
1670: Baroque altar-piece.
1683: Chancel decorated.
1697–1699: Addition of transepts.
1722: Transepts decorated.
1739: Vestry erected.
1752–1773: The church acquires a beamed ceiling, a new vestibule, steeple, font, and a Rococco pulpit (thought to be painted by Ezechiel von Dram 1763). The nave is extended to the west, the entire church heightened by four rounds of logs, and the walls painted blue.
1840: Shingled roof replaced by tile. Church restored.
The Rollag stave church is still in use.

beauty and faith. The majestic altar-piece at Rollag which gathers all of the ingredients of the Baroque period, memorializes its willing donors with the date 1670 and the initials "KISW" and "ISD" (Vicar Knud Jørgensøn Winter and his wife Ingebore Stephens-Datter) for all eternity. Later, Vicar Augustinus Flor's first initials and the year 1722 were added since he was responsible for the restoration of this altar-piece.

The church has another plaque which Winter paid for two years after becoming Rollag's vicar at the age of 35. The inscription relates that the panel was to be a reminder to himself and his wife and children to lead "the holy life". Winter, as was customary in his time, had "inherited" his wife, Ingebore Stephens-Datter from his two predecessors. The holy life must have agreed with Ingebore. She lived with her last husband for 31 years and also survived him by one year.

Another fine memorial in the church was donated by the widow of the Danish clergyman, Vendel, who spent 19 years of his life in this small, Norwegian outpost. A large portrait of his reverence Andreas Borch, vicar at Rollag from 1795 to 1816, crowns the clergy's own "testimonials" in this place of worship.

With its many additions and expansions over the centuries, little is left of the medieval stave church at Rollag.

The festive, blue interior with memorial plaques, portraits of clergy and an opulently decorated chancel.

FLESBERG

STAVE CHURCH

NUMEDAL

THE FLESBERG STAVE CHURCH welcomes you with a few remnants of its former glory, including a fine example of a medieval dragon portal. Little has survived from the Middle Ages in this panelled church which rests so serenely on an open and friendly field.

But when you enter the church, bear in mind that the nave is part of the original late 12th century stave church. This church once resembled the stave church in Borgund and those in Valdres. A painting of the church from 1701, hanging near the baptismal font, depicts the church in its prime with three naves, an exterior gallery, an apse furnished with a tower, and completely covered with shingling. The surroundings of the church have not changed. Large, upended slabs of slate from the 1600s still enclose the churchyard, and in the background the "infinite rows of slender pines stretching across the meadowland" are still in place.

The Vicar of "Flæsbergs Parish in Nummedal" in the 1730s, Johannes Bertelsen, did not seem to take much pleasure in the three churches he was destined to serve: Svene, Lyngdal and the parish church, the Flesberg stave church. In a document from 1732 found in the church archives, his complaints mention that the churches are small and "totally devoid of Structural Quality and Ornamentation". He wrote that the stave church was in the worst disrepair, and was so ancient "that it has existed since the Time of the Catholics ... No other Church owns Less and has more Need of Repair than the Parish Church." Vicar Bertelsen's situation was particularly difficult on major feast days when virtually the entire parish attended services, and also during "Catechization" which required him to "force my Way through the Congregation". Furthermore, the parish church had no vestry, and the communion rail around the altar was so little that "only 6 or 7 Persons can be served at the same Time".

Bertelsen's complaints were not in vain. Just three years after he wrote this document, the church was rebuildt.

Restoration activity has been constant since that time, and the most recent restoration between 1955–1965, gave the church its present appearance.

FACTS

Four or eight columned church, pentice and apse, probably from the late 12th century.
1683: Pulpit and baptismal font.
1700: Chandelier.
1735: Enlarged to a cruciform church. Free-standing posts removed. Flat ceiling installed and the church interior is painted by Ole Dahl.
1745: The church's first altar-piece installed.
1792: Copy of the old steeple installed in original place.
1802: Church interior painted by Kjetil Olsen Haugkjend.
1846–1848: Shingles on roof replaced with stone.
1870s: Extensive restorations, interior and exterior panelling replaced.
1900–1910: Church painted white.
1955–1965: Central Office of Historic Monuments directs interior and exterior restoration.
The Flesberg stave church is still a parish church.

This stave church has been the heart of the community since the end of the 12th century.

NORE
STAVE CHURCH

NUMEDAL

WHEN THE PARISHIONERS attended services in the Nore stave church in the 1700s, they may have had trouble finding available seats below the gallery in the north and south transepts. Here, the walls were covered with paintings of biblical sites – in riddle form. These puzzles were a guarantee against boredom, unless one was able to read or had not solved them during a previous service.

When Catholicism reigned and the mass was said in Latin, biblical murals served to educate the congregation, many of whom were illiterate. A few centuries later, the puzzles painted on the walls of the Nore and neighbouring Uvdal stave churches may have been more of a distraction than a focal point for concentration on the sermon. Apparently, the protestant clergy of Numedal believed that any pathway leading to the Lord was worth a try.

Judging by the beautifully painted floral decorations in three of the valley's four stave churches, it seems that pietism was an unknown movement to the people of this area. Here, the rustic arts were allowed to unfold, honouring God in spontaneous and brilliant colour. The Nore and Uvdal churches have many architectural similarities, but Nore has one distinguishing feature. This church had stave-built transepts terminating in apses as early as ca 1200. This is unique in the Norwegian church-building tradition.

The church nave, as it is today, has a second special feature. Two posts flanking the openings into the transepts divide the nave's longitudinal wall into three sections. These posts have plank traces showing that they had been used previously to support the side walls in the original transepts – the present log-built transepts were built in 1709 and 1714 respectively. As in a number of other churches, such as the one in Vågå, the man in charge of the reconstruction of the Nore church made use of material saved from earlier building stages. In the 1700s, a number of wall planks from the original transepts were used as floor boards in the new transepts.

The year 1880 could have been a fateful year in the history of the Nore stave church. Like many other stave churches at that time, the church had become too small. A new church had been built nearby, and a decision was made to demolish the old one. A few years earlier,

FACTS

Single-nave church from last half of the 12th century, with central mast, chancel, apse, pentice and bell turrets.
Ca 1200: Church acquires stave-built transepts each with an apse, and possibly with a *perivalium* (a conical roof surmounted by a round turret) like the Borgund stave church, the only known one of its kind in Norwegian architecture.
Middle Ages: Font and portions of two crucifixes from the 1200s.
1600s: Flat ceiling installed, transepts built, gallery constructed and chancel extended.
1655: Nave and chancel are painted. Pulpit installed.
1683: Chancel enlarged to its present size.
1704: Altar-piece with a painting of the Lord's Supper by Niels Bragernæs.
1700s: Major exterior and interior changes.
1890: Aquired by the Society for the Preservation of Ancient Norwegian Monuments.

The Nore stave church rests in an open valley.

architect Peter Blix had saved the Hopperstad stave church in Sogn from a similar fate. The Nore church was saved by professor Lorentz Dietrichson who was in the process of writing a book about stave churches. In 1888, after agreeing to assume responsibility for its maintenance, he became the sole owner of the church. He had managed to rescue the church, but two years later he was forced to rescue his personal finances by transferring ownership of the church to the Society for the Preservation of Ancient Norwegian Monuments.

In 1731, a new pedagogical tool was introduced in the Nore stave church: biblical sites presented in riddle form.

UVDAL
STAVE CHURCH

NUMEDAL

YOU HAVE NEVER seen such a garden! Luxuriant rows of roses, drooping branches laden with leaves, flowers in delirious colours.

Throughout centuries, seeds of faith have blossomed into a jubilant garden of praise in this tiny stave church at Uvdal. It would be difficult to find more beautiful accompaniment to the words of the Psalms and other biblical texts, which are painted with flourishing script on the church walls:

"... Then will I go unto the altar of God, my exceeding joy: yea, upon the harp I will praise thee, O God my God." (Psalms 43:4)

Ever since it was built on the location of an earlier church, sometime in the last half of the 12th century, the Uvdal stave church has been the subject of enlargement and change. Few of our stave churches can bear witness to such continuous development in the arts of architecture and decoration. The original church was extremely small with a total area of 40 square metres. The chancel, only 2.60 m wide and 2.40 m long, was enlarged both before and after the Reformation while the exterior gallery was torn down during the last major enlargement of the church in 1720. The original nave, the only section remaining from the 12th century church, now forms the nave's eastern section. The massive central mast, reaching from floor to roof-ridge, is still in this eastern section.

The Uvdal church also has west and south portals with medieval carving in a style much more akin to folk art than the "classic" stave church ornamentation. The church leaves many questions unanswered in terms of design, date and location. The western entrance portal, with carvings from the heroic Icelandic "Volsunga Saga" depicting Gunnar in the Snake Pit, is an eloquent introduction to the church's lavish interior. Eyes are literally drawn into a frenzy of sinuous vines before they are forced to stop abruptly at the dramatic red colour of the altar-piece and chancel table. The medieval posts flanking the chancel opening, which mark the original width of the chancel, are carved with some half masks which may have been intended to "nail down" evil spirits, but which are an unpleasant reminder of the existence of the devil even in this rose-painted place of worship.

F A C T S

Single-nave church from the late 1100s, with central mast, chancel, apse, pentice and bell turrets.
End of 1200s: Nave elongated to the west and a new mast added, apse torn down, and chancel extended.
1300s: Crucifix, probably carved by local artist.
1620: The first windows installed.
1624: Pews installed.
1656: Ceiling installed and interior decorated for first time in ochre, red, grey and white, by same artist who decorated the Nore stave church. Installation of pulpit, and possibly also the altar-piece depicting the Lord's Supper, by a local artist.
1684: Chancel extended to present-day size, new sections of interior painted to resemble earlier decoration.
1720–1734: Expansion to cruciform church, new bell turrets and vestibule. Pentice removed. New wall sections and panelling in gallery decorated by the "Painter of Blue".
1770: Pulpit and sides of pews decorated by "Painter of Green".
1819: Vestry added.
1901: Ownership of church assumed by the Society for the Preservation of Ancient Norwegian Monuments. The church is used once a month.

Many finds made during an archaeological excavation in 1978 beneath numerous layers of flooring attested to the fact that the congregation clung to ancient superstitions for a long time. Not only were items found that may simply have been lost during the church service, such as spectacle glass, fish hooks(!), jewelry, coins, crosses and pilgrim badges, but also unusual objects such as knotted cords and "pjotrposer", small cloth or leather pouches holding objects that were thought to have magical powers. It was believed that supernatural powers resided in the church and that possession of these talismans would enable them to influence these powers.

Beneath the church, mixed with building debris from construction and repairwork from previous centuries, were fragments of woodcarving and sculpture which had probably been discarded and replaced. Pieces of parchment also turned up, including a liturgical manuscript with musical annotation and illuminated letters, and a diploma from 1310 issued by Bishop Ketil in Stavanger.

To conclude in the concise words of Håkon Christie, "The Uvdal stave church is concentrated rural history in a picturesque framework".

Section facing the chancel. In the foreground, the massive central mast.

The church enjoys an open, panoramic view over the valley.

HEDALEN
STAVE CHURCH

VALDRES

HE WAS IN the depths of the deep forest, hunting with scant success when a large grouse fluttered up from a spruce tree. He released an arrow, and a moment later, heard a metallic sound, followed by the weak echo of a church bell. Had he come upon an enchanted bird? The huntsman followed the sound cautiously and deep in the forest, beheld his "prey" – a church. His arrow had glanced off a church bell. In keeping with the custom of the times, the huntsman made the sign of the cross.

"In the sacred Name of Jesus ..."

This is one version of the legend of the "discovery" of the Hedalen stave church in 1558. Hedalen had been deserted since the Black Death swept through the country in the mid-14th century. If the legend is to be believed, the forest had invaded the valley, concealing its church, farms, and settlements for nearly two hundred years!

When the huntsman came upon this small, single-nave stave church, and saw its pentice and magnificent west portal dating from the second half of the 12th century, it was just as the priest and his congregation had left it in the 1300s. The triptych with its graceful madonna sculpture, the soapstone font, and on the altar, the sacred vessel and reliquary of gilt copper had not been disturbed. But the huntsman found a bear hibernating at the foot of the altar. He killed the bear, and its pelt is still kept in the church's vestry. The poet Theodor Caspari, a precursor of environmentalism, warning against the decimation of our beasts of prey, wrote about the bearskin in the Hedalen church in his book *Fra Bygdevei og Sætersti* (1926):

"I have a suggestion: Soon, when the last bear in Norway, probably one from Hedalen, is killed by its fearless slayer, which will certainly happen, even if like its predecessor it takes refuge by the altar, then let this unchristian murder result in the replacement of the relic that is already in the church. I myself will extend even more reverence to this new martyr to the brutality of mankind."

At the Hedalen church social life was not limited to churchyard exchanges of gossip on Sundays and holy days. The main parish meetings had always convened during the feasts of Midsummer's Day (24 June) and Michaelmas (29 September). The inhabitants of

FACTS

A single-nave church from the 1100s, with no interior masts. The west portal is clearly related to the Hopperstad and Borgund stave churches, and dates the Hedalen church as an early one among the churches in Valdres.
Gallery and triple arch from the 1200s.
Madonna figure from the 1200s.
1699: Enlarged and converted to a cruciform church with log-built extensions. The original chancel, which according to sources from 1695 terminated in an apse in the east, was torn down.
1699: A pulpit is installed, decorated in 1776 by Hovel C. Gaarder.
1738: The church receives a new steeple which is erected by the famed church-builder Svend Olsen Traaset from Fåberg in Gudbrandsdalen.
1902 and 1908: Restorations. Services are still held in the Hedalen stave church every second Sunday throughout the year. It is also used for weddings and funerals.

According to legend, the Hedalen stave church was "discovered" in the forest in 1558, nearly 200 years after the Black Death.

Valdres, Hallingdal and Ådal met at the church for a few days of "all sorts of fun". Fighting and drinking were common ingredients of these festivities, although it has been said that their souls were so ingrained with respect for the church that their merriment seldom crossed the line of propriety. However, these celebrations came to a halt in 1860, among other reasons, due to strong pressure from the vicar.

The first recorded reference to the Hedalen church, possibly the oldest church in Valdres, is in a tithing directive from 1327. Like many other stave churches Hedalen was a church for votive prayers and offerings. There is reason to believe that gifts were plentiful; Hedalen's inventory, most of which is from the Middle Ages, is unusually opulent and generous. The pulpit from 1699 and the altarpiece are both remarkable for their fine ornamentation in fruit and flower motifs by Hovel C. Gaarder from Nordre Land in 1766. Also, the church's west portal is one of the definitive masterpieces of medieval art. Anders Bugge claims that the clarity and delicate composition of these dragon portals from the 12th and 13th centuries have no equal. He also maintains that the fighting dragons are not merely decorative, but that they symbolize "the collapse of the forces of evil in a self-destructive Armageddon at the very entrance to the hallowed place they had come to destroy".

Detail of the portal.

The chancel and its medieval altarpiece and crucifix. The crucifix has inspired the following words: "Here, pain is portrayed with greater reality than perhaps anywhere else in Norwegian art from the Middle Ages – and with an expression of the utmost beauty."

LOMEN
STAVE CHURCH

VESTRE SLIDRE IN VALDRES

AT ONE TIME, she must have had a body, perhaps even a child in her arms or on her lap. Today only her head is left and it shows signs of rough treatment. About 100 years ago, the head was fastened to the outside wall of the church, exposed to rain and snow. Guri Lome, who emigrated to America in the last half of the 1800s, told a neighbour that in her childhood this head had served as a "target" for local children's ball games. "The point was to get the ball into the crown."

The person with the crowned head belongs in Lom. Her name is the Virgin Mary.

The bubonic plague, which swept through the area in 1349, does not seem to have depopulated the community; historical documents suggest that the church has been in continuous use throughout the Middle Ages. The Virgin Mary, a source of comfort and consolation to the community in good times and bad, met her fate when the Reformation took over. The fact that her head survived can certainly be credited to her fellow villagers. The people of Valdres also viewed the new religion with deep scepticism; they were quick to remove religious paintings and similar forms of "Papist Corruption" from sight. This fine early gothic sculpture, as old as the church which was built between 1180 and 1250 – researchers use wide margins here – is presently in place on the altar of the Lomen stave church. Even though the head might not receive the same religious deference that it once enjoyed, it is still rightfully considered an historical treasure.

Other medieval inventory from the early days of the church includes a chest inscribed with runic symbols which is very similar to the chests found in the Oseberg viking ship excavations, a prayer stool, the base of a font and a tapestry which may have been used as a wall hanging or as a burial shroud.

The church has undergone numerous reconstructions and restorations over the years. Originally it may have been similar to the stave church in Torpo. Both of these churches belong to the "masted stave church" of the Borgund or Sogn/Valdres type: a high structure without exterior galleries, a small chancel, vestibules on the west and south entrances, one or two bells above the central section, and a shingled roof. The Lomen church is also similar to its nearest neigh-

FACTS

Masted stave church, 4 corner masts from ca 1180–1250, with chancel, apse, and vestibules on the west and south entrances. The central section of the church is the original section.

Two church bells from 1200 and 1300 respectively.

Chest with runic inscriptions, possibly from the Viking Age.

1200s: Head of a Madonna sculpture.

1200–1300: Tapestry.

Ca 1200: Portals.

1600s: Bell turrets.

1628: Altar-piece, probably painted by the well-known Valdres artist Ola Hermundsson Berge in the late 1700s.

1628: Pulpit, possibly painted after a major restoration in 1789.

1674: Belfry.

Ca 1750: Central section enlarged. Slate roof installed, the new walls panelled horizontally, and the chancel expanded to the width of the original central section.

1797: Church rebuilt.

1842: Church rebuilt. Posts, arches, beams and cross braces (St. Andrew's crosses) painted pale, dusty pink; walls in nave and chancel painted green; ceiling painted grey-white.

1960s and 1970s: Church restored, pink paint removed.

bour to the north, the Høre stave church, which also falls into the Sogn/Valdres category. However, the construction techniques in the Lomen and Høre churches are more advanced, since the weight of the roof is supported by fewer masts. Of the church's 14 masts, only its 4 corner masts reach to the floor. The other 10, 3 on the long sides and 2 on the short sides, stop at the ceiling and the weight they support is buttressed by semiarches between the corner posts. The ancient portals on the Lomen and Høre churches are similarly designed, but although the two churches were built by the same master builder and team, the portals were not carved by the same artist.

The improved standard of living in the 1600s benefitted the church too. Repairs and acquisitions mentioned in the financial accounts of the Lomen stave church during this century show clear signs of prosperity. But as early as the mid-1700s a systematic rebuilding of the church was undertaken "due to a State of Decay". Herman Ruge, then vicar of the church, expressed his doubts about this project which he believed was ruinous "to a Devotee of ancient Architecture, of which this was a great Masterpiece". During a later rebuilding in 1842, things went from bad to worse. It is sufficient to say that among other things, the church's interior was painted in dusty pink, green and grey-white. In a final restoration, undertaken between 1960–1970, the pink colour was removed, but despite the church board's recommendation, the green and grey-white colours were preserved. The Director of Historic Monuments wanted the church to be an illustration of how taste changed over the years.

Nevertheless:
"Small and brown and safe she appears
with a belfry sounding her call.
The bells have pealed a thousand years
and here most beautifully of all.

"Small and brown", the Lomen stave church rests safely beneath the towering Lomisberget.

HØRE
STAVE CHURCH

VANG IN VALDRES

"THEREAFTER KING SVERRE went up to Valdres and took rightful lodging at his farms."

This account of the king's visit to the valley in 1177 comes from "Sverris saga". Whether he visited the large Kvie farm in the community of Høre is not certain but this may have been the year that Elling, Master of Kvie, and his brother Audun joined King Sverre's men. Erling Jarl (also called Erling the Lame) and his son Magnus Erlingsson fought against Sverre. Two years later Erling Jarl fell in the Battle of the Calfskin at Nidaros, and the two brothers then agreed to build a church in Høre. The following runic inscription carved into the supporting stave inside the pulpit in the Høre stave church attests to this fact:

"The summer when the brothers Elling and Audun ordered cutting (trees) for this church, Erling Jarl died in Nidaros."

This inscription has led most researchers to agree that the stave church was consecrated in about 1180. The first recorded mention of this church is in 1327 where it is called "ecclesia de Ordun".

The church is situated on a hillside close to the many buildings belonging to the Kvie farm, a farm that is oftened mentioned in Norwegian history. Gyda, the proud woman who was to become Harald Hårfagre's future queen was raised by the Master of Kvie, and it was from Kvie that she refused the king's request, sent by messenger, to be his mistress. A few hundred years later, Kvie reappears in history. Ragnfrid, the daughter of Elling of Kvie, had married the mighty Bård of Rein in Trøndelag, and the wedding is thought to have taken place in the newly-raised Høre stave church. The couple had many children, including Duke Skule, who was raised by his mother's father, Elling of Kvie. The fight for the crown in the first half of the 13th century between Duke Skule and King Sverre's son's son, Håkon Håkonsson is recounted in Henrik Ibsen's drama, "The Pretenders" (1863). Invaluable coin discoveries beneath the church floor, dating as far back as 1040, indicate that the Høre stave church and the Kvie farm have been important religious and trading centres throughout the 1200s.

FACTS

Masted stave church with 4 corner posts, chancel, apse, and pentice from ca. 1180.
End of 1600s: Altar-piece, presently hanging on the north wall of the chancel.
Ca 1750: Chancel rail.
Ca 1800: New altar-piece and pulpit made by Tomas Tomasson Tørstad.
1822–23: Church expanded, pentices, original chancel and apse removed.
1828: Chancel rail, altar-piece and pulpit decorated by painter Gullik Knutson Hovda.
1857: The belfry is given its present form. Portions of the old bell turret are incorporated into a churchyard gate.
1901: Churchyard enlarged.
1905: Memorial stone erected in honour of Harald Hårfagre's Gyda.
1930: Baptismal font made by Christoffer T. Kvien.
1979: Archaeological excavations and restoration.
The church is still in use.

Altar-piece from the late 1600s.

As is so often the case, the existing Høre church is the second one on the same location. Archaeological excavations in 1979 uncovered earthed posts for a little church from about 1100. It was probably torn down because of its state of decay, at about the same time that the present church was built. The excavation uncovered many finds similar to those made in a comparable investigation on the site of the Uvdal stave church in Numedal, including numerous objects that had been lost by the church-goers over the centuries. Of the many grave finds made beneath the church floor, traces of child burials and "embryo packets" are considered most interesting.

The Høre stave church and the Lomen stave church which is a little farther south in the valley, may have been built by the same master, although the dating for the Lomen church is less precise, estimated between 1180–1250. Both churches belong to the Sogn/Valdres group. These churches have four corner posts and powerful arches supporting the other posts on the long and short sides. Painter J.C. Dahl believed that the builder had been inspired by Byzantine architecture. Today however, experts have found that at that time there was a general trend toward churches designed with fewer posts.

Today, portions of the ancient bell turret adorn the churchyard gate.

ØYE

STAVE CHURCH

VANG IN VALDRES

ALONG THE MAIN road in Øyebakken, in Valdres, there is a small stave church, "Ecclesia de Obdal" – the Church in Oppdal – or, as it is officially called today, the Øye stave church. Stout and secure, it seems to have risen from the ground it stands on, but this is not the case. Originally it was in another location.

Few of our stave churches have been more secretive about their past, provoked more questions from our experts, and provided fewer answers than the Øye church – so far. Similar to many other stave churches, the first time that Øye is mentioned in a written source is in 1327, in a papal messenger's tithing directive. However, the church was probably built in the 1100s. A runic inscription inside the church reveals that it was consecrated on September 29, but the year is not mentioned. Since St. John the Baptist died on September 29, the Øye stave church was probably dedicated to him.

As mentioned above, the church was moved from its first site on the level fields by the Vangsmjøsi Lake – a building site which, to put it mildly, would prove to be unfortunate. When the river flooded, which it did quite often, the groundwater rose, half-filling the graves in the churchyard with water. When a burial took place in a flooding season, stones had to be placed on the casket before it was lowered into the ground.

The proximity of the lake may have also been unfortunate in that it caused the church to decay. In any event, in about 1740 the decision was made to demolish the church and erect a new log-built church at Øyebakken, a higher location. By 1747, the church's days were numbered. Out of respect for the old church, some of its logs were used in the new structure, and one of its portals was installed in the new vestry. In 1866, this portal was given to the University Museum of National Antiquities.

No one knew what had happened to the rest of the old church until almost 200 years later. In 1935, when the walls of the new church began to split, the craftsmen who were repairing it found the materials from the old church. They were carefully stacked beneath the floor of the church – 156 pieces, which were duly registered by the Central Office of Historic Monuments and stored until a recon-

The chancel, 14th century crucifix, and exceptional wooden font.

struction of the church was initiated in 1960.

It is difficult to place the Øye stave church in a category. Its exterior resembles two of the five other stave churches that still exist in Valdres, the churches in Hedal and Reinli, both of which are single-nave churches surrounded by pentices. However, the interior of the church raises, in the true sense of the word, problems. There are four free-standing masts placed close to the corners, as in Høre and Lomen, but unlike these two churches, the masts do not penetrate the roofing in a raised central section. The masts are braced across the room with a broad string beam which is supported by complete arches between the masts, and semi-arches against the outer walls. There is only one other church that has this particular type of construction – the Vang church, which was torn down in 1841 and moved to Riesengebirge in Germany (now Poland).

Had the Øye church been altered before it was torn down in 1747? The amputated keyhole-shaped portal may suggest that it was. In addition, traces on one of the masts indicate that the church once had a steeple. In this case, the masts may have penetrated the roofing to support a raised central section.

The stave church from the 12th century was dismantled in 1747 and re-erected in 1960–1965, using much of the original material.

HEGGE
STAVE CHURCH

ØSTRE SLIDRE, VALDRES

HIS SINGLE OPEN eye stares straight ahead, his mouth is distorted into a grimace, and he sticks out his tongue scornfully. This grotesque head, one of ten masks decorating the tops of the columns, is a distinguishing feature of the Hegge stave church. These heads, or masks, which are also in a few other stave churches, have presumably had a function beyond the purely decorative. One of many theories suggests that they were meant to keep the evil spirits in their place. Unlike masks found in other churches however, experts such as Anders Bugge maintain that the one-eyed mask in the Hegge church represents a definite person, the Norse God, Odin.

What is this god of heroes and strong men doing in the temple of the White Christ? Were the old pagan gods still wielding some remnants of power when this church was built in the first decade of the 13th century, 200 years after Christianity came to Norway? Obscured in anonymity, and disguised by the fact that Odin was forced to support the church roof here, this "portrait" can easily be seen as a tribute to former gods. The fact that Odin is sticking out his tongue in God's house is also thought-provoking – although our former Director of Historic Monuments Roar Hauglid has pointed out that figures sticking out their tongues are a familiar Romanesque motif in other churches, both in Norway and abroad.

Whether or not this represents Odin, it has seen many generations come and go, and watched the church interior shift in pace with the mood of each century. In 1864 however, when a ceiling was installed above the nave, the masks on the columns were hidden from the congregation. Today, they can only be viewed from the belfry. All that remains from the medieval church's main section is the skeleton of a stave church with eight interior masts. The rust-coloured medieval framework is clearly profiled against the church's bright green vertical panelling and grey ceiling. The bright walls also provide a fine, neutral background for the magnificent 17th century pulpit and opulently carved altar-piece from ca 1782 in which the Last Supper is a central theme. According to tradition, this altar-piece was donated to the church by four cattle traders from Hegge who had come into bad weather on their way to Gudbrandsdalen. They were lost in the fog,

FACTS

Eight-masted church of the Valdres type, probably built in the first half of the 13th century. Often mentioned in written sources, first in 1322. Originally with a pentice on all sides.
Early 1200s: West and south portals.
Ca 1200: Baptismal font.
1600s: Pulpit.
1782: Triptych carved by Østen (Øystein) Guttormsen Kjørn.
1694, 1706 and 1712: Reconstructions.
1807: Restoration and enlargement by church builder Johs. Korpberget from Gudbrandsdalen.
1844: Church enlarged, including a new choir (chancel).
1864: Addition of vestry and ceiling.
1923–24: Restoration.
1930s: Belfry and gallery erected under the direction of architect Arnstein Arneberg.

Exterior and interior of entrance portal.

which did not lift until they promised to donate an altar-piece to their local church. In Skåbu, they met the renowned woodcarver from Skjåk, Østen (Øystein) Guttormsen Kjørn – also called "Kjørrin", the name of his cotter's farm. He is said to have learned the art of woodcarving from the nestor Jakob Bersveinsson Klukstad, a master of variations on the acanthus design.

The four men went to fetch their altar-piece in the spring. After their rugged journey over crusty snow, they saw that Judas had fallen off the sled. When Judas was found, supposedly many years later, the apostle's red tunic was greatly faded, but the priest would not allow a restoration. He maintained that the weak shade of red was the right "Judas colour".

The church's soapstone font, which is thought to be from Vågå, is badly scarred around the edges. According to legend, small pieces of soapstone were secretly chipped off the font and placed in a camphor solution which was said to cure all sorts of ailments.

Much of the church's medieval appearance was lost during two comprehensive restorations in 1807 and 1834. However, two portals carved in vine and dragon motifs from the early 1200s are still in place. The interior entrance portal has a beautiful metal door-ring, lock and key dating from 1200–1250. Should you lift the door-ring, do so with reflection and humility. This ring was held during the taking of an oath. Also, many a persecuted person saved his life in the old days by managing to catch hold of the door-ring. Touching the ring guaranteed the same right of asylum as being inside the church.

The Hegge stave church is the parish church in Østre Slidre.

The Hegge church with its post-Reformation belfry. Hegge is the only remaining stave church and medieval church in Østre Slidre.

REINLI
STAVE CHURCH

SØR-AURDAL

"She is ancient, the Reinli Church,
yes, many hundreds of years.
The little people moved her
to where she now appears."

The Reinli stave church is about 40 kilometers north of Hedalen, overlooking the Valdres valley. According to legend, credit for this magnificent location can be given to the underground creatures. In fact, the church was originally at the base of the valley, a location which must have annoyed the "little people". In the course of one night, they transported the church far up onto the hillside, where it is today. They must have been rather sceptical of Christianity. Legend also relates that during the first service held in the church, a wood nymph stood at a high place, Langeberget, and played such a wistfully beautiful song on her horn that the congregation was compelled to leave the church in wonderment. However, a defender of the faith appeared in the unusual guise of a ram which rushed after the nymph, goring her to death.

The earliest mention of "Reinlidar kirkja" has been found in the records of a papal emissary in 1327, but it is likely that the church was built as early as the 1200s by Sira Thord, who carved his name on the floor of the church gallery with the following runic inscription: "Here rests Sira Thorder who built this church. Pater Noster." Beneath this rune, five iron nails (two are missing today), forming a Latin cross, mark his place of burial. During an inspection of the church in the 1950s, a man's skeleton was found half a meter below the floorboards. It is believed that these are the earthly remains of Sira Thord.

The design of the single-nave Reinli stave church is unique. The chancel and nave are the same width and form a single room terminating in an apse with the same diameter as the church's entire width. The church is clearly inspired by the European Gothic hall churches, such as Saint Louis' Sainte Chapelle, in Paris. The elegantly carved posts and pilasters enhancing the church's three portals are also unquestionably influenced by Gothic stone architecture. In this church, dragon carvings are conspicuous by their absence.

FACTS

A single-nave church with 6 posts set into the walls, probably dating from the 1200s.
Unusual design, inspired by the continental Gothic hall churches such as Sainte Chapelle in Paris. The chancel, nave and apse are the same width. Pentice and apse probably a later addition in the Middle Ages.
Ca 1200: Romanesque soapstone font. May have belonged to the second church at this location, which was destroyed by fire.
Twelve consecration crosses from the Middle Ages.
The altar-piece is a modified triptych, probably as old as the church. Its panels from the 1920s were painted by Siwerts.
Renaissance pulpit in the same style as the Hedal stave church pulpit, probably by the same woodworker. The ornamentation – fruit and flower motifs in strong colours – is also the same style found in the Hedal church.
Crucifix, carved in the 17th or 18th century, modelled after medieval crosses.
1870–80: Belfry erected.
1977–79: The Organ restored.
The Reinli stave church is only used during the summer months.

Looking toward the chancel, showing the modified triptych from the Middle Ages, and the Renaissance pulpit.

Many interesting finds were made during excavations in 1971–72, including a charred layer showing traces of an earlier church that had been destroyed by fire. Below this layer, an even older burial ground was found, with remains of men, women, and children. In all probability, a church was here when these people were buried. It is likely that the Reinli stave church is the third church to have been built on this location.

Reinli is the only church in Norway that still has all 12 of its consecration crosses from the Middle Ages. When the inventory and gallery were removed during the 1971–72 excavations, more of them were uncovered. All of the crosses (each 30 cm in diameter) were placed at a height of 220 cm and probably date from Sira Thord's time.

In fact, we can thank Reinli's local inhabitants for the fact that the stave church is still there today. After the "little people" left the church in peace, time passed quite undramatically. But in 1734, the church was threatened by its own vicar! He wanted to build a new church and managed to convince twelve of the area's most important farmers to set their seal to a document which included the statement that a new church was necessary because it "was in extreme disrepair and in a dilapidated state from foundation to roof" and there were no more craftsmen "familiar with so-called raised timber construction". The vicar gained the support of both the king and the bishop, but met strong resistance from the local inhabitants. Although he managed to build his new church, the original one, which the older generation just 50–60 years ago still referred to as "Old Guri", was left in peace.

Meticulous restoration has made this church a wondrous sight, one that delights many. Sira Thord, who is still at rest beneath the gallery, is certainly pleased too.

"Reinlidar kyrkja" was probably built in the 13th century.

TORPO
STAVE CHURCH

HALLINGDAL

HERBRAND COULD FEEL his neighbour Gunnar breathing down his neck. It made him uneasy and the priest's sermon, coming from the lectern, required concentration. Herbrand and Gunnar had long been engaged in a bitter dispute about an outlying field. Neither of them was willing to make a concession of any kind. But it was probably he himself who had right on his side? "Thou shall love thy neighbour ..." Herbrand sighed. It was difficult to be a good Christian. He looked toward the altar, toward the burning torches that cast their flickering light over the altar's sacramental vessels and illuminated the painted decorations on the massive baldachin over the altar. He saw Christ enthroned and encircled by his apostles before his gaze continued down the sides of the vaulting where the martyrdom of St. Margaret of Antioch was depicted in ghastly detail. Margaret is scourged, dipped into boiling oil, shown hanging by her hair – all for the sake of her religious convictions, for refusing to give in to the pagan emperor Olybrius. But Herbrand can also see Margaret's triumph: God's own hand draws her into heaven while the devil collects Olybrius' soul. Such was Margaret's courage and faith. Perhaps he, Herbrand, should heed the Bible and "turn his other cheek" to Gunnar. He sang the final psalm joyfully with the congregation.

An unknown artist painted these "graphic scenes" from St. Margaret's life in the Torpo church almost 800 years ago. It is doubtful whether the lessons from these scenes touch our souls in the same way, but the colours, painted in distemper on chalk, have kept their radiance and strength down through the years. However time has not been as kind to the church itself, which was once the parish church of Ål. On an arcade plank dating from the original church, about 1200, the master builder and his group of men have proudly carved their signatures: "Toralf built this church, Asgrim, Haakon, Erling, Paal, Eindride, Sjønde, Torolf, Tore carved, Olav."

The stave church that these men built was a columned basilica with an exterior gallery, chancel and apse. Today the church is sorrowfully abbreviated, with neither chancel nor pentice. It has been rightfully said that it is more like a belfry than a place of worship. Nevertheless, the church interior is a good example of advanced stave

FACTS

Masted stave church with pentice, chancel and apse, built ca 1200, probably on the location of an older church from the early 1100s.
1250–1300: Lectern and baldachin. Some of the lectern probably removed after the Reformation to make room for a pulpit.
1628: Installation of the two first glass windows.
1632: New or rebuilt ridge turret.
Early 1800s: Exterior gallery removed.
1880: Chancel torn down.
Ownership of church assumed by the Society for the Preservation of Ancient Norwegian Monuments.
Service is held each year on St. Olav's Day. The church is also used for weddings and funerals.

The national highway "Riksvei 7" runs past this little church.

church construction with the nave columns dividing the space into a central section and four side areas. In fact, the removal of the chancel and pentices provides a clear picture of the basic idea of a high-ceilinged central section with a saddle roof and a lower aisle section with sloping roofs. We can only imagine how the chancel with its main altar once were. A panelled wall has been installed in the chancel arch, but the arch is still supported on each side by a delicately carved capital. Material from the chancel was saved and used in a new church that was built to the north of the stave church in 1880, where the belfry once stood. The stave church's two medieval bells also found their way to this new church. However, the benches along the walls of the nave, as well as the floor boards have remained in the old church since the Middle Ages. The magnificent south and west portals are also from the early days of the church. Their carving is similar to the Urnes style, but there are some innovative elements. The dragons have acquired wings, and the Christian vines are sprouting healthy new leaves.

Traces of an even older church on this site have been found here too. Carving designs on a plank thought to come from this former stave church portal resemble those associated with the Urnes style. Therefore this earlier church can be attributed to the early 1100s.

The baldachin portraying the life of Jesus and the martyrdom of St. Margaret.

GOL
STAVE CHURCH

HALLINGDAL
(A copy of the church was built in 1994)

(Now in the Norwegian Folk Museum at Bygdøy, Oslo)

"IT FELT SO empty when they no longer could be heard ..."

The same church bells had been ringing over the Gol community for hundreds of years. One day in 1847, they fell down and broke beyond repair.

This event was to symbolize the future fate of the church. Torjus Finnesgarden (Hagen), holder of a large farm, and Sexton Haavelsen were the owners of the church but they refused to replace the church bells unless the municipality also contributed. They protested in spite of the fact that in their capacity as church owners they were expected to be responsible men, that is to say land-owning farmers with enough wealth to cover the expenses of the church. It deserves to be mentioned that none of Gol's church owners had paid attention to this requirement since the early 1800s.

Not only had the Gol stave church begun to show signs of deterioration, it had also become too small for its steadily growing congregation. In 1846, steps had been taken to improve the graveyard, which had also become somewhat too small. The graveyard was surely an eerie sight in the years that followed. Lack of space was so critical that it became necessary to dig up relatively new graves. For many years, remains of corpses and coffins in the graveyard were "placed in Sight of All, which in Truth must have upset and pained all thinking and feeling Christians".

A last, major inspection of the church was undertaken in 1876. The conclusion, that it was "in a piteous state," led to the erection of a new church. In 1882, the old and venerable "House of God" which had "risen over the community for 700 years" was dismantled. Its remains were transported over snow and ice to Gulsvik, shipped by boat over Lake Krøderen in the spring, and finally sent by rail to Oslo. In 1884, King Oscar II lay the cornerstone for the reconstructed church at Bygdøy (Oslo), and the church has been there ever since.

Although it was built in the mid-1200s, the first recorded mention of the Gol stave church is not until 1309, as "Gardar kirkja", and in 1328 as "ecclesia de Gard". In its present reconstruction, the church is similar to the Borgund stave church. Although the reconstruction

FACTS

Masted stave church from the mid-1200s with 14 masts, 8 of which reach to the floor.
1200–1300: Church bench from the Heddal stave church in Telemark.
13th century: Carving and inscriptions in chancel.
Ca 1650: Decorative painting in chancel and apse in Renaissance style, in red-brown, ochre and pale blue on a whitish background with typical strong black contours and lines.
1882: Church dismantled.
1884: Church rebuilt at Bygdøy (Oslo) by architect W. Hansteen, under the supervision of antiquarian N. Nicolaysen.
Protestant and Catholic services are held during the summer months.
A copy of the church has been built at Storeøini, near state highway No. 7, just outside the centre of Gol.

The following text appears within the painting:

Hiere hauer iog bies min sunder. Alde liuens sloe af huis hundles naade vnd Frider syket in og hild Synsemisker viis og hos Gom i verdens minde Fra holder enig onsolds Bos Gra min første Forin og Gst Gom ies iemis af din fil Imin Moders siuog Barin blef ies vid din Naadof Vor m

Desse Ferde for ieg saer Frøys Gar Gey paa himlen goe Brode noi Furren fra Imin spade Barn doms Grand For min Jum mer Barie gav du mire af moders Brysk som med saerlig hus ble kryst Imin ungdom dagiig Brod ies hos Tus og aue nod

Hav Søe o gud vor Geader mand for sia eng war sam er vars hoy Sa du rette siusens fred La prale aand omiis vore sin og gud, til vore øyer vind gud farte oppaa os arine smaa Gom i din forsyns øyt søe du undsf hvor den vor Sire eagien stal seieris for os al vor dad ain Syse Hetlered iv e ga ti

1699

---

was based on knowledge about the original church and available historical sources, the church was also partially modelled on other parish churches. Sections copied from the Borgund church included the belfry, the dragon heads on the gables and the exterior gallery. The supporting skeleton with its masts and most of its supporting beams, a third of the wall planks, and one of the portals all come from the original church in Gol. The ground plan of the church is similar to the Hegge stave church in Valdres, with eight longitudinal masts and large arches bridging the cornerposts of the nave in the east and west. The dragon portals in these two churches are also similar, and the masks topping the masts bear enough resemblance to those in the Hegge church to allow for the assumption that they were carved by the same artist.

The ornamentation of the church was financed by two government officials and a number of successful farmers. *The Book About Gol* relates the following:

"We know that many of those who were a part of financing the artwork in the church were certainly not the most unobtrusive in manner and mood. On the contrary, many of them were fined and censured for fighting and bloodshed and many kinds of lawbreaking."

This painting from 1699 is now at the Norwegian Folk Museum at Bygdøy. It was originally donated to the Gol stave church by the farmer Bjørn Frøysaak, portraying himself and his family.

The Gol stave church, re-constructed at the Norwegian Folk Museum at Bygdøy, may be the church that receives most visitors.

HØYJORD

STAVE CHURCH

ANDEBU

LIKE SO MANY other churches, this one was hidden behind panelling and pietistic white paint for well over 200 years, and was not particularly remarkable. The "book was judged by its cover". When the Director of Historic Monuments conducted a church survey in 1905, a stave church appeared from behind the panelling.

Høyjord, or "Haugagjerdi", the only stave church that has been preserved in this area of Norway, was built in two different centuries. The Romanesque chancel dates from the late 12th century, while the Gothic nave was added about 100 years later. The church has 12 supporting posts or staves, all of which are different. The church probably had a central mast at one time, which might have been added when it was rebuilt in about 1690. Church accounts from that time record an order for "1 Mast for the Tower, 24 *Alen* (about 16 metres), 8 Inch Top", measurements that could suggest a central mast. A central mast of this kind symbolized Jesus, while the 12 other posts were to symbolize the apostles.

During a restoration of the church in 1948, everything that was not a part of the original stave church was removed. This process uncovered a foundation stone for a central mast, justifying the construction of a new central mast.

More exciting medieval discoveries were also uncovered, including traces of decorations in the chancel and 8 to 10 consecration crosses on the walls. A consecration cross, evidence that the church had been consecrated by the bishop, was a small cross enclosed in a circle painted in tar. In Christian symbolism, the circle of eternity and the cross are joined. During the time of Roman Catholicism, this was an established ritual at every church consecration. The bishop, who was always present, applied consecrated oil to 12 crosses that had been carved into the wall previously. A candle was lit beneath each cross, symbolizing the apostles who spread the Christian faith throughout the world. The crosses were then painted as visible proof that the church had been consecrated. These consecration crosses had three functions: to keep evil spirits away from the church, to show that the church belonged to Jesus Christ, and to remind the congregation of His suffering and death on the cross. Major repairs, restorations, or

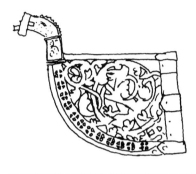

FACTS

Single-nave church with 12 posts and central mast.
Late 12th century chancel; nave from the latter half of the 13th century.
Eight to ten original consecration crosses.
Carved altar-piece in the "Jarlsberg Renaissance style" by a woodcarver who worked between the 1630s and 1640s.
1689: The church is modified, ceiling installed and pentice torn down.
1782: Baptismal font.
1848: Pulpit.
1948–53: Restoration supervised by architect Otto L. Scheen.
1960: The church's altar-piece and rich medieval decor is restored by Finn Kraft.
The church is still in use.

Høyjord, Norway's southernmost stave church, is north of Sandefjord and west of Tønsberg.

desecrations necessitated a new consecration ceremony, and if older crosses were ruined, new ones had to be made.

During the restoration, five well-preserved skeletons of a man, two women and two children were found under a thin layer of soil beneath the chancel floor. These were probably buried here during the Black Death in the mid-1300s. Other finds included a stick carved with 51 runes and the inscription "Ave Maria gratia plena" (Hail Mary full of grace), and 52 silver coins, most of which were Norwegian.

The carved altar-piece in the "Jarlsberg" Renaissance style dates from 1630–1640s.

RØDVEN
STAVE CHURCH

ROMSDAL

WITH ITS DIAGONAL supports protruding like long legs from the body of the building, the Rødven stave church looks like it is clinging to the soil. It is reminiscent of a giant marooned insect, or a dog, trying to get its legs in place on slippery ice. The church, almost on the shoreline, faces directly into the wind from the Romsdal and Rødven fjords, and has had to withstand many a storm. The entire church suffered severe damage in the storm of 1689 when its tower and roof were ripped off and blown into the fjord. It was not until 1712, under the direction of Vicar Thomas von Westen, that the church was properly repaired.

The present appearance of the church dates back to this reconstruction. Here, as in Kvernes and many other stave churches, the nave and chancel are all that remain of the original medieval stave church. The nave, with inserted intermediate posts on its long walls, and the distinct gothic characteristics of the south portal, and otherwise unlike all other known stave church portals, may date from about 1300. The north portal however, flanked by pilasters with Romanesque details could be considerably older, probably from the late 1200s. No traces have been found of older churches on this site, but coins dating from the 1200s that were found here suggest that the present church has had a predecessor.

Latin letters reading "consecrated 16 October ..." can be seen on a severed wallplank used in later years to cover a former window opening in the nave's north wall. However, the rest of the date has disappeared. Consecration crosses have been found on other planks, but these have not helped researchers determine when the church was built either. Runic inscriptions have also been found in the church. One of these, "To God will I", may have been carved by one of the many worshippers making a pilgrimage to Nidaros by the ocean route. Then as now, the church's most special attraction was a life-size crucifix from the 1200s, which was said to work miracles. With the exception of the crucifix the interior of this church is characterized by the post-Reformation period.

Formerly, church earnings from their properties were to be applied, among other expenses, to repairs and ornamentation. It was the

F A C T S

Single-nave church with inserted posts on the longitudinal walls. Thought to have been built ca 1300. The medieval church had an pentice on all sides, but this was torn down during a reconstruction in the 1600s. It is not known whether the external diagonal supports are from the original church or whether they were added at a later date.
End of 1100s: Northern portal with Romanesque details.
1200s: Crucifix.
Ca 1300: South portal with distinct Gothic characteristics.
Ca 1600: Chancel restored.
Ca 1650: Walls and ceiling decorated.
1651: Vestry.
1712: Altar, altar-piece and pulpit
1712: Church reconstructed by Hans Knudsen from Molde.
1715: Altar-piece painted.
1791: Baptismal font.
Ca 1824: Large windows on lower level installed.
1908: Church ownership assumed by the Society for the Preservation of Ancient Norwegian Monuments.
Service is held on Midsummer's Eve. The church is also used for baptisms and weddings.

king's responsibility to see that this was carried out. However, after 1660, monarchs began to dip into these funds to pay for their wars. Consequently, churches often fell into decay. Frederik IV solved his financial problems by auctioning off more than half of the country's churches to private persons. The highest bid won the church; the new owner's identity was unimportant. At a public auction in Trondheim in the mid-1720s, as many as six churches in Romsdal, including Rødven, were sold with all their property and tithes. Councilman Lorentz Holst became the new owner of Rødven.

The new owner of a church was meant to assume responsibility for the church's condition. But sometimes the vicar himself, if he could possibly afford it, stepped in when he thought the church needed renovation or when he wanted to decorate the church in honour of the Good Lord. Gifts from members of the parish were also welcome. The altar-piece from 1712 in the Rødven church was painted in 1715. An inscription relates that this was done at the expense of a fellow clergyman at the Veøy church, Otte Jacobsen, and his wife Inger Margrethe. This couple also had the altar draped in red material on which their names were embroidered inside a garland of flowers.

Once inside, one's attention is drawn toward the life-size crucifix on the northern side of the chancel door. This is probably from the mid-1200s and is considered a masterpiece.

The new late-19th century church can be seen behind the old church from ca 1300.

ATHANAS:

CONSENSVS FIDEI CHRISTIANORVM EST INTERITVS DIABOLORVM:
ITEM: SINT VNVM MANEANT VNVM, PATEANTVR ET VNVM
QVI VNVM DE CHRISTI NOMINE, NOMEN HABENT:

ANNO 1633 Haffuer Anders Erichen Pastor till Quernes gield, till guds æriß
forfremmelse oc hanß kiere Sogne folck till villie oc tienifte paa Egen bekoftning, afft
nij lade opbijgge det offuerfte Choer, met ftoele, vinduer, oc maßning, faa vell
som dett nederfte Coer, met vinduer oc forten, formed fuende ftoeler for hæm
medt folck, med dett meige.

pfalm 93:
Din Vidnisbijrd, ere Saare troofafte, Hellighed er ditt
Hußis prijdelse Herre
Euindelig:

KVERNES
STAVE CHURCH

NORDMØRE

THE SACRED PLACE was high and prominent, easily visible to all who sailed or rowed in from the fjord or the islands further out at sea. People had been coming here to Kvernes since time immemorial to worship their gods and bury their dead.

Weather was harsh here, but vessels could always find shelter on one or the other side of Lundanesset, depending upon whether the wind came from the southwest or the north. Although the forces of nature changed little or not at all, the centuries left their mark on the human spirit. Eventually, man turned away from the "sacred white stone", demolished the pagan temple, and replaced it with a building honouring a new god called Jesus Christ.

No one knows how long a church has been at Kvernes, but the existence of the present stave church is documented by Archbishop Aslak Bolt's rent book in 1432. At the earliest, estimates date the church between 1200–1300.

Like so many of our stave churches, all that is left from the original church is the main nave, which is 16 metres long and 7.5 metres wide. However, unlike most familiar stave churches, in addition to its cornerposts, its long walls are divided into sections by intermediate posts. Outside the church, external diagonal props, "skorder" along the southern long wall provide additional support for the weight of the roof. It is likely that both long walls once had these props, but whether or not they were part of the original construction is unknown.

The numerous reconstructions and extensions of the Kvernes church bear witness to the fact that Kvernes must have been an important religious centre, especially in the 17th and 18th centuries. The first reconstruction in 1633 included a new chancel (same width as the nave), and a baptistry. Anders Ericksen or Anders Quernes, a name he also used (vicar of Kvernes from 1603 to 1662), played an important role in the formation of the richly decorated interior. A painting on the church's northern wall by painter/portraitist Johan Hansen Kontrafeier depicts a church under construction and bears the following inscription:

"In the year 1633, to promote the honour of God and to please

FACTS

Single-nave stave church with two inserted intermediate posts on each long wall, and corner posts. Built at the earliest between 1200–1300. First mentioned in written source in 1432. Only the nave remains from the medieval church.
1475: Altar-piece, Baroque mounting installed in 1695.
1633: Chancel torn down and new one erected in notched log construction in the same width as the nave. Stave-built baptistry erected. Nave entrance moved from the west to the south. Painted decorations on chancel walls and ceiling.
1640–1650: Wall and ceiling of nave decorated with painted acanthus designs.
1648: New steeple erected.
1652: Pulpit from the Netherlands installed, donated by Vicar Anders Ericksen.
1690: Rood screen.
Ca 1730: Baptismal font by Peder Knutsen Kjørsvik.
Service is held on Midsummer's Eve. The church is also used for baptisms and weddings.

Memorial painting, by Johan Hansen Kontrafeier, honouring the restoration of the church in 1633.

and be of service to his beloved parish, Anders Ericksen, Vicar of Kvernes parish, at his own Expense, has ordered the addition of seats, windows, and painted decorations in the upper Chancel, as well as windows, and font, in the lower Chancel, and even two chairs for visitors, with the personal mark ..."

The "personal mark" is Anders Ericksen's own and it is also on the sides of two church benches and, with his initials, on the coat of arms of the dual kingdom of Denmark/Norway hanging behind the pulpit.

Upon the death of Vicar Anders Ericksen, who is said to have been a very wealthy man, a memorial plaque was placed in his name in the chancel by his widow, "the respectful Matron Lisbet," in tribute to her "honourable and learned Spouse".

Of the church's rich inventory, the altar-piece is in a class of its own. From about 1475, it reflects a merging of Catholicism and Protestantism, and depicts the Virgin Mary and her mother, "Anna herself" holding the Christ Child on her arm. The altar-piece, paid for by Vicar Hans Hagerup, is in a Baroque mounting from 1695, and includes portrayals of Moses with the Ten Commandments and Christ with the banner of victory.

In spite of its exposure to the open sea, this ancient place of worship, like the Grip stave church, has withstood all storms and remains firmly in place. It even escaped being torn down in 1893, when a new church was to be built. As a curiosity, it should be mentioned that no less than three future bishops in the Church of Norway have been christened in the Kvernes stave church.

The Kvernes stave church and its characteristic "skorder", diagonal props supporting the southern wall.

GRIP
STAVE CHURCH

NORDMØRE

THE ANGRY WAVES beat against the island, greedily devouring its barren rock shore before lashing out against homes and out-buildings. The storm from the northwest gains momentum and attacks this small island, savagely shaking, ripping and tearing at the irritating land mass so stubbornly inhibiting its freedom to sweep freely across the open sea. The island's inhabitants, mostly families of impoverished fishermen and coastal pilots, have taken refuge in the church on the highest point of the island, eight metres above sea level. Generation upon generation has sought spiritual redemption and security in this church.

They huddle together in the freezing church; draughts seep in through the walls and windows, and the candle flames leap and flutter horizontally. All look toward the beautiful altar panel depicting the Virgin Mary, Saint Olaf and St. Margaret – who provides protection in storms and is the patron saint of seafarers. Perhaps someone in the group is thinking about the person who gave this triptych to the church more than 300 years ago, a young Dutch princess who had also experienced anguish and spiritual desperation. This is the story:

A fleet of 11 ships set out for Copenhagen from the Netherlands on July 15, 1515. One of the passengers was the 14-year-old Princess Elisabeth of the Netherlands/Spain, the future bride of Christian II, King of Denmark-Norway. Another passenger was the Archbishop of Nidaros, Erik Valkendorf.

A terrible storm blew up during their passage. The young princess was extremely sea sick and extremely frightened. Was she to die during her journey to the strange country in the far North? If she presented a gift to the church in Norway, would the Good Lord take pity on her soul? She sought the advice of the archbishop, and they devised a plan. Shortly after the princess' safe arrival in Denmark, an order for five identical triptychs was sent to Utrecht in the Netherlands. The altar panels arrived in Norway five years later, and Erik Valkendorf placed them in his own diocese, in Ørsta, Hassel, Røst, Leka and, in the Grip stave church.

The night-time storm on Grip in 1796 washed nearly 100 buildings into the sea, and three persons lost their lives. But the stave

FACTS

Single-nave stave church built ca 1470. One of Norway's smallest and most simple stave churches. The chancel and nave are of equal width.
1520: Dutch triptych.
1621: Church restored and rebuilt.
1600s: Decorations and inscriptions.
1860–70: Church restored. New windows installed and inner walls panelled and painted white.
1932: Church restored. Inner panelling totally removed, outer panelling partially removed. Interior restored to its original style. Exterior walls covered with rough panelling, asphalt shingling and vertical panelling painted with tar, oil and caput mortuum in a reddish-brown colour. Services are held every third week during the summer.

church kept her occupants from harm and survived the tempest as it always had and always would.

Neither storms nor tidal waves, but modern society finally managed to wipe out the small island community of Grip, 14 kilometers from the coast of Norway. Until the island was incorporated into the city of Kristiansund in 1964, it was Norway's smallest municipality with a permanent population of 135 persons. Today, it is abandoned. To some people, Grip is an island of memories and ancestors; to others it has become a summer paradise, a "strawberry trove", an island of summer homes.

The Grip stave church was probably built in about 1470, slightly more than half a century before the Reformation created turbulence in the life of the church. It is one of our smallest and most unassuming stave churches, and with the exception of the Dutch triptych, it has always been modestly equipped. Originally, the triptych could be closed with hinged panels, and like all Catholic artifacts, the enthusiasts of the Reformation insisted upon its removal. Here too, the inhabitants were also resourceful and managed to hide their unusual treasure. The triptych was not replaced in the church until the 1932 restoration – and without its door panels. A beautiful and rather unusual chalice from 1320 is also part of the church's medieval inventory. The post-Reformation church interior includes painted draperies and twining vines as well as a number of biblical figures. Passages from the Bible in Danish and Norwegian Gothic script decorate the crossbeams. The decorations are most likely the work of local artists.

During the summer season, services are held in the church about every third week.

This little stave church at the mouth of the fjord has withstood storms for hundreds of years.

HOLTÅLEN
STAVE CHURCH

GAULDAL

(Now at the Trøndelag Folk Museum in Sverresborg near Trondheim)

"THE PEOPLE OF HOLTÅLEN and other barbarians" were the words of the Pope in Rome. According to tradition, God's representative on earth associated the people of Holtålen with barbarians because of the following episode which is said to have happened during the "Catholic Era".

It was a bitter, wintry night when a little child was to be baptized in the Holtålen stave church. When it was time to administer the Holy Sacrament, the poor priest discovered that he had forgotten to warm some water, and there were no stoves in the church. It was hard to find a solution, but the priest had a bright idea. He asked the flock of parishioners to spit into the baptismal dish. This they did, and the child was duly baptized. Since this was not exactly a baptism according to the rules, the event was reported to the Pope. In his great mercy, he did not allot any punishment. But – and this is how the parishioners got their name – "Holtålinger and other barbarians" were told that this "was not to repeat itself".

The people of Holtålen must have been bitter about being branded in such a negative way. They were probably no worse than others. The parish was a large one, farms were far apart and distances between the farms and the church were often great. His Holiness had no way of understanding that warm water was not always available in the twinkling of an eye. Furthermore, he might not have been so quick in his criticism if he had known that this little stave church in Trøndelag owned one of Norway's oldest and finest altar frontispieces, the "Olaf antemensale" which is now in the Nidaros Cathedral.

"Holtaalls kirkja" is first mentioned in 1345 but it is much older, possibly dating from the 1100s. In all likelihood it was a very simple building with a combined nave and chancel, a typical example of very early stave church architecture. Little is known about the church during the Catholic Era. However in 1642, a document stated that the church was in disrepair, its income was minimal, and worst of all, "the clergy was neglectful". Exactly ten years later, the situation had clearly improved; altar-piece, baptismal font and pulpit were decorated by the renowned painter from Trondheim, Peter A. Lilje, also known as Peter Kontrafeier. These must have been among the last

FACTS

Single-nave stave church, possibly built in the 1100s. Original south portal. West portal from ca 1200, from the Ålen church.
Middle Ages: Consecration cross
1604: Painted decorations (fragments).
1652: Altar-piece, font and pulpit painted by Trondheim artist Peter A. Lilje, also known as Peter Kontrafeier.
1704: Church moved, new nave built.
1881: Church dismantled.
1884: Reconstruction of church at the Trøndelag Folk Museum in Sverresborg, near Trondheim.

The west portal, originally from the dismantled Ålen church. The capitals on the two shorter masts decorated with the "water-leaf" motif.

improvements since by 1703, Vicar Johan Lobes was already complaining that Holtålen as well as other churches in the parish were "very ancient and totally unsuitable". All of the churches had certainly become too small for the steadily growing population, and in 1704, the Holtålen church was moved down to the river. Here, a new nave was built, and the old church was used for the chancel and vestry. Nevertheless, the church was still dank and cold, and still without heat. It must have been in poor shape. The church was so poor that it has been said that hoes and shovels were kept at the entrance because "for many years, the parishioners had to dig the graves for their deceased themselves".

In 1884 the church was moved to the Trøndelag Folk Museum in Trondheim. Here, a new west wall was built and the west portal from an old, dismantled church in the neighbouring parish of Ålen was installed.

Holtålen is one of Norway's smallest and most rudimentary churches. The rectangular nave is ca 5 x 6 metres, the chancel, 3 x 3.5 metres.

GARMO
STAVE CHURCH

GUDBRANDSDALEN
(Now part of the Maihaugen Collection, Lillehammer)

WHEN ST. OLAV was travelling up and down the valleys of Norway spreading Christianity, his most important missionary tool was the sword. However, for reasons unknown to us, not everyone was threatened with fire and weapons. Torgeir the Old from the Garmo farm in Lom was one of those who was able to negotiate with the king. He was offered Lake Tessevann, a lake rich with fish, if he accepted the Christian faith and built a church on his farm. This is the legend. It is also documented in a manuscript from the 1200s.

Torgeir converted to the new religion and built a church, and Lake Tessevann became his. So much is certain. But whether it is his church that is at Maihaugen in Lillehammer is another, very controversial subject. Some believe that the oldest wall planks could come from the time of Torgeir the Old, but Roar Hauglid, former Director of Historic Monuments, has stated that the church's oldest sections are most likely from the late 1100s. Archaeologist and museum director Sigurd Grieg, who became Director of Maihaugen after Anders Sandvig in 1946, has indicated that evidence from the former church site at Garmo may show post holes from a former stave church, the one that Torgeir had built.

There are those who confront the present-day Garmo church with scepticism and insist that it has been thrown together from mixed material of highly questionable authenticity. Maihaugen's "father" Anders Sandvig made no secret of the church's doubtful origins. When it was decided to demolish the Garmo church in 1880, since it no longer satisfied modern requirements for a church, this old house of prayer was put up for auction. Attending the auction was the omnipresent Vågå man, Trond Eklestuen a local character who went around the valley buying "junk". He was to become Anders Sandvig's "official purveyor". One of Sandvig's books recounts that the Garmo church was appraised at 200 kroner. "But Trond could only guarantee 160 kroner." However he bought anything he could afford, "including the construction framework, the beams, some staves, sections of the roof, a dragon head, font, altar-piece and pulpit". Many parts of the church were spread to all corners of the country, and some of them were also burned, but due to detailed records from the auction,

FACTS

Single-nave church with corner posts from ca 1200.
Stave-built nave, chancel and vestry of equal width. Chancel may have been narrower, perhaps with an apse. The church may have had an exterior gallery until 1689–90 when a major reconstruction took place under the leadership of Vicar Bendt Friis M.A.
Ca 1100: Soapstone font.
1690: Spire and bell tower.
1695: Altar-piece: "made and painted" by Sigvard Guttormsen, presented to the Lillehammer stave church by Colonel Georg Reichwein. Crowns and "wings" in acanthus ornamentation, probably carved by Bjørn Olstad from Øyer in 1732 when the altar-piece was moved from the demolished Lillehammer stave church to the new church in Lillehammer.
Ca 1730: Pulpit from the Hustad church in Romsdal.
1882: Church removed from the Garmo Farm in Lom.
1921: Church reconstructed at Maihaugen under the direction of architect Jürgensen.
Service is held on Midsummer's Eve. The church is also used for baptisms and weddings.

enough material from the church was gathered to enable the reconstruction of the Garmo church at Maihaugen in 1921.

The Garmo church looks very much like the real thing to the uninitiated. But what did the church look like before it was reconstructed at Maihaugen?

A sketch by Joachim Frich from 1850 shows a cruciform church with a stave-built nave, notched-log transepts and a bell tower with a tall spire and four smaller pinnacles. The original Garmo church was probably very plain, having little decoration and no particularly distinguishing features other than its dragon head and ridge capping.

Most of the original church inventory has been lost. Some of it can be found in the Lom stave church. The Garmo church has only kept a small painting and the medieval soapstone font, but it has other furnishings that have been garnered from a number of churches in the valley. Among these "borrowed" treasures is the altar-piece that decorated Lillehammer's church from 1695 until 1880 which had been found in a shed on the Hammer Farm and bought by Sandvig for 300 kroner in 1886. The altar-piece was the first of Sandvig's purchases, and this is how he tells the story:

"I felt so terribly sorry for that altar-piece hidden in the carriage shed ... For hundreds of years it had been the finest decoration in the old cruciform church, generation after generation had turned toward this piece in times of sorrow as well as joy. Now it was discarded, lying like some old piece of junk in a carriage-shed, available to anyone who wanted to buy it."

The stave church from the Garmo parish in Lom has been given a worthy location at Maihaugen. From this new location, one can still hear "church bells chiming over the memory of bygone generations".

The altar-piece from 1695 in the Garmo church was originally in the Lillehammer stave church, before this church was torn down. The pulpit, from ca 1730, comes from the Hustad church in Romsdal.

VÅGÅ
STAVE CHURCH

GUDBRANDSDALEN

"The Vågå church is shy and small
though her graceful contours we find.
On hallowed soil her timbers tall
reveal the Old Norse mind."

WHEN COMPOSER DAVID Monrad Johansen left St. Peter's Church in the Vatican in Rome after his first visit there, he turned to his Norwegian friend and cried out in surprise: "The church at Vågå is a beauty!"

In a mysterious way, the stunning sensual impressions from Christianity's greatest monument awakened the memory of his first visit to the Vågå church. So beautiful, so small – but so grand – and created by the inhabitants of a small mountain settlement. At this first visit he had not made any comparisons to other churches. When Monrad Johansen left the church, he was overtaken by tears.

The colour of golden honey, the Vågå church rests on "an agreeable place in the beautiful community of Vågå". Vågå's "Vatican church" known once as "Ullinsynjar kirkja a vaga" had been gathering people for prayer and meditation for many centuries. But Vågå had also been the centre of worship in northern Gudbrandsdalen long before Christianity and the "Hvitekrist" arrived in Norway. The area supported more than one pagan temple, often belonging to the many large farms which were, and still are, plentiful in Vågå. Kvarberg, Sandbu, Blessom, Valbjør, Håkenstad ... these ancient ancestral estates still lie scattered along the hillsides. When the King of Norway, Saint Olav, brought Christianity to the valley in 1021 temples were probably hastily torn down and replaced by churches. The king left no room for doubt: Christ or death. Tradition relates that he himself ordained the first priests in Vågå as well as in the neighbouring community of Lom. There is good reason to believe that there was a church in Lom as early as the 11th century. But according to Snorre's saga the king indicated that it would be a sin "to burn such beauty". A similar threat may have haunted Vågå and Lesja. At any rate, all three communities were quick to convert to the Faith.

FACTS

Single-nave church with no interior columns, probably also without pentice or apse.
1100s: Soapstone font.
1200s: Crucifix.
1627: The church is torn down and rebuilt as a cruciform church by Werner Olsen, who makes use of materials from the original church as well as from another stave church. West and south portal as well as the west wall's blind arcades remain unchanged.
1630s: Octagonal Dutch Renaissance pulpit.
1674: Altar-piece by "picture carver" Johannes Larssen Skraastad from Vang in Hedmark.
1677: Altar-piece and pulpit painted by "portrait painter" Peder Jonsson.
End of 1600s: Painting depicting the Fall of Man on the north wall by the Vågå clergyman, Henning Munch.
Ca 1700: Paintings in vestry.
1600–1700: Belfry. Bells are from the 19th century.
1914: Restoration supervised by architect Heinrich Jürgensen.
The church is still Vågå's main parish church.

The altar-piece is encircled by luxuriant acanthus designs, also called "the French leaf".

After Urnes, Vågå is thought to be our oldest stave church. It is estimated that Vågå was built between 1100–1130 although there is no recorded mention of it until 1270. Originally, Vågå was probably a rather small single-nave church, showing traces of Norman architecture, without interior columns and possibly without an exterior gallery or apse.

In 1627 the church was in such disrepair that it had to be torn down. However, it was respectfully reconstructed with careful attention to style by Werner Olsen, who was able to use some of the material from the original church. The west and south portals and the fancifully carved blind arcade on the west wall remained in place. Some sections of the animal ornamentation on the portals are reminiscent of the Urnes style. Only the Vågå and Urnes churches have a series of blind arcades, and these two stave churches are also the only ones with carving done directly on the wall planks.

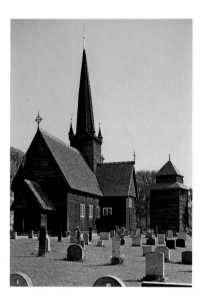

The Vågå church has a natural setting in the centre of the community.

The interior of the church is just as inviting as its bright and welcoming exterior implies. The rich colours of the Middle Ages and the linear simplicity of the Renaissance meet and join the new Baroque style which literally cries out from the gilded acanthus vines encircling the altar-piece and climbing the chancel arch with luxuriant escutcheons and memorial plaques.

A magnificent Gothic crucifix from the 12th–13th century hangs over the fanciful chancel arch, and is all that remains of the old church's inventory. The crucifix hangs on a crossbeam once called "the excommunication beam" from the days of Roman Catholicism. When a priest excommunicated a sinner, he was to have stood beneath this beam. In the most lenient form of excommunication, the sinner was allowed to enter the rear section of the church, but could never step beyond this beam.

Throughout the centuries and right up to the present, the builders and artists of this town and valley have placed their special mark on this lovely place of worship. Vågå's artist Trygve Håkenstad is responsible for one of the church's two chasubles.

The Vågå graveyard which has numerous graves from the 17th and 18th centuries, and deserves a chapter of its own, inspired Norwegian artist Erik Werenskiold's "A Farmer's Burial" and his first version of this painting comes from this churchyard. Soapstone memorials carved with acanthus vines flourish in competition with the natural flowers of the area. Many of the memorial stones are the work of "stoneworkers *anno domini*" such as Østen Kjøren, Anders Aasaamoren and Jacob Sæterdalen. Contemporary artists have also left their mark on this graveyard. Painter Kristen Holbø, himself from Vågå, has designed a beautiful gravestone for his parents. Gerhard Munthe is responsible for the monument to Vågå's most legendary citizen, the reindeer hunter Jo Gjende.

RINGEBU
STAVE CHURCH

GUDBRANDSDALEN

A JOURNEY TO Ringebu in search of God's word "neither driving nor riding" but walking, will strain both legs and lungs. The Ringebu church is on a high hillside setting. Not an unusual location, in fact. Tradition has also played its role in Ringebu, and in all probability the location had been used for cultic worship in pagan times. An open area to the west of the church, *Gildevolden,* was the site for legislative and judicial assemblies in the Middle Ages.

In 1928, the renowned regional historian Ivar Kleiven from Vågå wrote in his book about Ringebu: "According to sources trusted by the experts, the church was built before 1270 since it was first mentioned in a manuscript from that year. Therefore, the church could stem from Magnus Lagabøter's time, but there is no evidence disproving that it might be 60 or 70 years older." This statement is one that can also be trusted by contemporary experts.

In the Middle Ages the ancient trail taken by kings and pilgrims to Nidaros passed through Gudbrandsdalen. Many a pilgrim received a blessing in the Ringebu stave church. Two runic inscriptions have been found in the church, and one of them may have been carved by a local inhabitant:

"Here he was, and from here he departed."

The pilgrims savoured the memory of this richly ornamented church as they continued northward. The most beautiful sight here may have been the statue of St. Lawrence. His mild, forgiving gaze, and the inscription from the legend of St. Lawrence, "Night carries no Darkness for the one who knows the Divine Light," were certainly a source of hope and comfort for those about to set out on such a difficult and dangerous journey.

The St. Lawrence statue from the second half of the 13th century, may be the work of the little-known artist, "Balkemesteren". Not only has this wooden figure withstood the ravages of time, it has also managed to avoid the purges of the Reformation and remains securely in its place in the church. Among the church's other treasures are a 12th century soapstone font and two crucifixes.

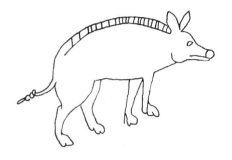

FACTS

A 12-masted stave church.
Built in the 13th century, probably before 1270.
The nave is all that remains of the original church.
Ca 1630: Expanded to a cruciform church. A separate free-standing belfry. The steeple, with its soaring spire and pinnacles (smaller towers flanking the main tower), is the work of Master Werner Olsen who was responsible for the reconstruction.
1686: The church adds an altar-piece, executed by Johannes Lauritsen Skraastad.
1703: A pulpit is erected, executed by Lars Jensen Borg.
1922: The ceiling from 1630 is removed and the nave regains its original medieval character.
The Ringebu stave church still functions as the local parish church.

The restoration of the church after the Reformation bears witness to the fact that Ringebu was a prosperous community. The post-Reformation inventory includes the carved altar-piece (1686), which is thought to be the work of Johannes Lauritsen Skraastad, as well as the pulpit, and Fredrik IV's double monogram above the chancel rail, both of which date from 1703. The royal monogram and sections of the pulpit were carved by Lars Jensen Borg from Christiania who introduced Baroque acanthus carving techniques to Gudbrandsdalen during his travels in the early 18th century. Although church restorations and decorations represented considerable expense, the congregation contributed generously. There was no lack of wealthy benefactors who probably hoped their memorial plaques and gifts would be "For the Honour of God and the Beautification of the Church", but who were not averse to having their names inscribed permanently on the walls of the church. Among the gifts from the vicar at Ringebu from 1695–1705, and Thomas Randulf, Gudbrandsdalen's district magistrate, was the royal monogram. A contemporary writes that "the august vicar, Otto Ørbeck" also provided sculptors and portraitists "with room and board for a considerable length of time, at no expense to the church ...".

Many late 17th century headstones and plaques are still in the church graveyard. One especially beautiful stone commemorating Margretha Irgens, a clergyman's wife who died in 1767, is probably the work of the district's famous woodcarver and artist, Kristen Listad, "The Flower-Master of Ringebu", as he was often called.

The Ringebu stave church can thank many benefactors from the post-Reformation era for its opulent interior decoration.

The slim, soaring – and now red – spire is the distinguishing feature of this columned "basilica".

LOM
STAVE CHURCH

LOM

A RUNIC INSCRIPTION can still be read on a cross brace in the triforium of the Lom stave church:

> "I have done the work of 2 men"

These runes are believed to date from about 1150–1200, when the church was under construction and the scaffolding still in place. They tell of the builder's pride in his work and his belief that the inscription would bear witness to his skill for centuries. He probably believed that nothing could threaten a church that was to be consecrated to the Blessed Virgin, John the Baptist and St. Olav.

Our medieval man was right. Lom's stave church still stands in the heart of the community, under the soaring mountain, "graceful and beautiful on the sandy plain above the Otta River". And it is still an important structure, the spiritual heart of the area today as it was almost 800 years ago.

According to tradition, the first priests in Loar (Lom) and the neighbouring settlement of Vågå were ordained by St. Olav during his missionary journey through the valley in 1021. In fact, post holes found beneath the Lom church may indicate that a church had been on this site in the 11th century.

The Lom stave church's architectural composition and numerous other details testify to the fact that western Norway was not far away. Therefore, the church is categorized as a "West Norway Church" in the Kaupanger group.

Generation after generation has put its mark on this church in accordance with the philosophy and taste of the times. Perhaps not always with the same success. For example, the medieval delight in form and beauty, expressed so richly in its architecture, religious art, textiles and silver, was literally obliterated by the men of the Reformation. Out went altar-pieces and triptychs, artwork and sacred vessels. Some were thrown into the Bøvra River, some simply plundered. In came dark panels solemnly inscribed with the fundamental doctrines of Christianity.

Such a radical change was not easy for the public to accept over-

FACTS

A masted stave church from the early 1200s. Pentice, from the second half of the 1200s, has been removed.
1634: Log-built addition.
1663: The church assumes a cruciform shape and a new tower with tall, thin spires is added. A flat, raftered ceiling is installed throughout the building. The work was done by Werner Olsen.
1700s: The church obtains paintings by the Vågå artist, Eggert Munch.
1793: The church adds a pulpit and chancel arch.
1933: Under the direction of Architect Hustad, the church is restored to its original medieval appearance.
1965: The original ridgetop, with its cross and dragon's head, the only surviving examples of roof decorations from the Middle Ages, are replaced with replicas. The originals are placed in the Sandvig Collections, Lillehammer.
The church still functions as the local parish church.

The angels flanking the Baroque altar-piece were carved by two young men from Lom in their hope for mercy after they deserted in the war against Charles XII.

night. Tales circulated about priests having to pay with their lives – for the glory of God! – because of their purges.

By the 1600s however, a general reaction to these bleak churches initiated some changes. Even within the clergy, "absolute dogma" was easing up. Decorations appeared in the nave as early as 1608, and after this the tendency toward ornamentation gathered momentum until far into the 18th century. Two masters of the folk arts that were flourishing so abundantly in Øvre Gudbrandsdalen were commissioned: the Baroque scroll woodcarver Jacob Rasmussen Sæterdalen from Lom, and painter Eggert Munch, son of a clergyman from the neighbouring area, Vågå. Local inhabitants willingly donated funds to pay for these decorations, but the angels flanking the altar-piece came to the church in an unusual way. Two young boys from Lom who had joined the war against the Swedish king, Charles XII, deserted and fled to the mountains to avoid a death penalty. While in hiding, they indulged in an unusual pastime: they each carved an angel for their local church. After a while they ventured back home with their wooden sculptures, and were pardoned after entreaties from the local villagers.

The Lom stave church was restored in the early 1930s. The original medieval construction was "liberated from its flat ceiling and whitewashed walls," from 17th century Pietism, and its "barnlike" windows were replaced with small-paned windows with green glass. The Lom church has provided the background for many important occasions, such as the Sunday in July 1928 when the Norwegian vespers "Te Deum Laudamus" were first sung. They were based on folk tunes from Lom, collected and arranged by musicologist O.M. Sandvik, and adapted for choral song by the composer Sparre Olsen. For the first time since the Middle Ages, antiphonal singing between clergyman and choir, and choir and soloists, could be heard in the Lom church.

This vesper service may have been similar to those heard by the masterbuilder of the Lom church in the 1200s who, according to tradition, is buried in the church's graveyard. The poets Olav Aukrust and Tor Jonsson, two other local citizens of renown, also rest here. Tor Jonsson set the community and its inhabitants in a perspective of eternity in these lines of verse:

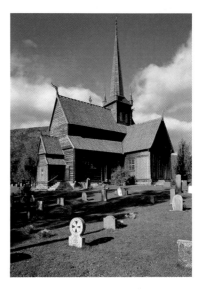

The Lom stave church, which is still the main parish church, has been in continuous use since the early 13th century.

> The timeless mountains rise and soar,
> red rays from a constant sun pour
> over peak and crest.
> And those to whom I raised my spear
> are born of the same blood and fear,
> and have the same unrest.

LIST OF PHOTOGRAPHERS

THE REBUILDING OF STAVE CHURCHES

Fantoft Stave Church

A stave church in Fortun in Sogn, dating back to the 12th century. It was dismantled in 1879 and sold to Consul F. Gade in Bergen who, in 1884, had it re-built at Fantoft, just south of Bergen. It was then restored to what was believed to be its original design, using Borgund Stave Church (see p. 17) as a model. The original church bells from the old Fortun Stave Church were used in a newly built church on the same site in Fortun, whilst a shrine from the 13th century was moved to the historical museum in Bergen.

In 1916, the Fantoft Stave Church was sold to Jacob Kjøde, a shipowner in Bergen.

During the night of 6th June 1992, the Fantoft Stave Church was completely burnt down. In 1993, the Kjøde family started the rebuilding of a copy of the church, using the foundations of the previous one.

A large stone cross, which stands outside the church, dates from around the year 1000.

Gol Stave Church

The original stave church from Gol (see p. 73) has been reconstructed and today stands at the Norsk Folkemuseum in Oslo. A copy of this church has been built at Storeøini, near state highway No. 7, just outside the centre of Gol. Storeøini was the centre of this community during the Middle Ages.

The new Gol Stave Church was consecrated on 10th July 1994.

© Boksenteret Erik Pettersen & Co. AS, 1993
Fifth edition 2001
Published in cooperation with Fortidsminneforeningen
Editor: Stein Winther, Redaksjonskontoret
Translated by Ann Clay Zwick
Picture research: Svein Thygesen
Graphic design: Eia Grødal
Drawings: Bjørg Omholt
Map: Ugland Totalkart AS

Desktop-published by Boksenteret AS
Reproductions: Offset Kopio, Helsinki
Printed by: New Interlitho, Milan, 2001

ISBN 82-7683-011-0